IMA

CW00449770

Around
Gillingham

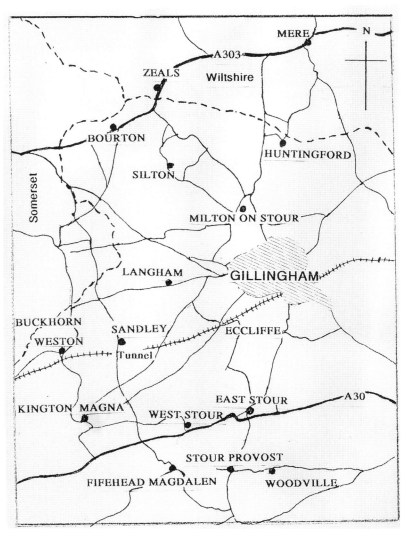

Gillingham nestles in the northern tip of the county of Dorset, just two miles from both Somerset and Wiltshire. This map covers an area of approximately five and a half miles by eight.

IMAGES OF ENGLAND

Around Gillingham

David Lloyd

NONSUCH

First published 1998
This new pocket edition 2006
Images unchanged from first edition

Nonsuch Publishing Limited
The Mill, Brimscombe Port,
Stroud, Gloucestershire, GL5 2QG
www.nonsuch-publishing.com

Nonsuch Publishing is an imprint of Tempus Publishing Group

British Library Cataloguing in Publication Data.
A catalogue record for this book is available from the British Library.

ISBN 1-84588-273-3

Typesetting and origination by Nonsuch Publishing Limited
Printed in Great Britain by Oaklands Book Services Limited

Contents

Acknowledgements

My special thanks go to Peter Crocker, chairman of the Local History Society, and Lyn Light, the honorary curator of Gillingham Museum, who have helped and encouraged me to complete this project, as well as my wife, Kathy, and sons, Andrew and Richard, for their endurance, assistance and understanding throughout the collection and preparation stages. Special thanks must also go to my father, Cliff, and late mother, Ivy, who helped so much with the identification of so many people in the group photographs.

I am also grateful to the following people and organisations that have loaned photographs, helped put names to faces and supplied other information:

Betty Allard, Tony Allard, Dick Arnold, Philip Arnold, David Ayles, Nick Baker, Nigel Bennett (Lloyds Bank), Mervyn Biss, Carola Bland, Mr and Mrs Sam Braddick, Bill Budden, Maj. Gen. Carrick, Bob Carter, Hilda Collier, Bruce Cook, Malcolm Cross, Mrs C. Cox, Ted Cull, Michael Dacre, Peter Daniels, Elaine Davis, Anita and Raymond Dear, Mr V. Duffett, Mr and Mrs Elsworth, Mr and Mrs E. England, Bertha Francis, Mr and Mrs R. Gallbally, Mr Gatehouse, Gillingham Museum, Gillingham School, Mrs P. Grace, Mrs D. Gray, Herbert Green, Owen Green, Les Gurnett, Mrs K. Harris, Mrs P. Hicks, John Hillier, Sonia Hillier, Di and Ken Hiscock, Robert Hooper, Don Hoskins, Alan Hoy, G. Herbert Hoy, Marion Hughes, Ivy Hull, Joan Jaggard, Beryl Knapton, John Knapton, Herbie Light, Mike Lloyd, Sue Lodge, Gordon Luffman, Jean Male, Jesse Martin, NatWest Bank, Roy Ozzard, Peter Mera, Jeffery Pink, Jess Pitman, Vic Pitman, Richard Phillips, Mr and Mrs Eric Proudley, Mrs V. Raymond, Phil Read, Mrs V. Richards, Rosie Roberts, Janet and Philip Robson, Michael Rose, Pat Rugman, Robert Smith, Mr and Mrs R. Stacey, Rex Standerwick, Ken Suter, Tommy Suttle, Mrs L. Taylor, Mr and Mrs Ken Taylor, Bill Trim, Phil and Peggy Wiseman, Sam Woodcock.

Thanks also go to those of you whom I have omitted to mention. Copies of photographs unused on this occasion will be saved for a future project and/or passed on to the Gillingham Museum.

Please send any correspondence relating to any of the photographs to me, c/o Gillingham Museum, Chantry Fields, Gillingham, Dorset SP8 4UA, or e-mail at Davidlloyd @ btinternet.com.

David Lloyd, 1998

Introduction

In 1992, I helped Peter Crocker, the chairman of the Local History Society, with his book of Gillingham photographs and I commented that there was plenty of unused material – 'You can do the next book', he said. So here it is – a collection of nostalgic photographs, mostly taken from my own personal collection, supplemented with images from Gillingham Museum and private archives.

To compile such a book has been a long-held ambition of mine, initiated by an interest in photography, family and local history and a fascination with Reece Winstone's Bristol books (produced many years ago prior to today's surge of interest in nostalgia). It was eventually Peter Daniels, a photographer and the author of several Salisbury books, who inspired me to 'get on with it'. My roots in Gillingham go back a long way! My great-great-great grandfather was married in St Mary's church in 1820 and all generations since, bar one, have been married in the same place. The average age of all my grandparents was ninety-nine, so I learnt a lot from their memories, an experience which helps when studying local history.

~Gillingham is fortunate in that there were photographers around to record the people of the town and the many, often gradual, changes to the buildings, shops, etc. Adam Gosney and Charles Johnson were studio photographers up until the beginning of the twentieth century. When Edgar Samways used to run out of postcards, he popped out of his shop and took some fresh photographs, which he did right up until the 1930s. W. Phillips of East Stour was prolific with his plate camera, particularly in the Stour villages, whilst Ernest Berry's photos cover the 1930s and 1940s. It was around this time that cameras were developed for personal use – although the quality of Box Brownie photographs are not up to the standard of those taken by experts, such as Johnson, Samways and Berry. However, life was recorded and many of the results are represented in this book. At this point I shall issue a plea to those that are custodians of the family photos – please record the date, the event and names on the back. The memories fade rapidly, so do it now!

~It has often been said to me that Gillingham is not a pretty place and certainly not a tourist attraction. Whilst it does not have as many historic and picturesque features as its close neighbour, Shaftesbury, it does have a great variety of architectural features for the discerning visitor to find. Unfortunately, two great fires in 1694 and 1742 destroyed over forty houses – who knows what great buildings were lost? However, the purpose of this collection is not to feature old buildings, such as Great House, the Malt House or the humps and hollows of King's Court (one of King John's houses), but to concentrate on areas, such as the High Street.

The virtue of this approach is that the reader can appreciate the changes and revel in nostalgia, with the added advantage of seeing the people who have lived and worked in the town and surrounding villages.

At the beginning of the seventeenth century, Gillingham was still a small village. The present High Street consisted of houses and dwellings of the period with at least two inns, the Red Lion and The Phoenix. The Free School was a large building near the church. Its most famous pupil was Edward Hyde, First Earl of Clarendon (1609–1674), who was the father of Queen Mary II and Queen Anne. Robert Frampton, who was later to become the Bishop of Gloucester, was elected headmaster of the school in 1648.

Despite its rural setting, Gillingham could claim to be an industrial town. In 1769, the Gillingham Silk Co. established the silk-throwing industry (i.e., the process of preparing raw silk for the weaver). In the early years of the nineteenth century, around 160 people were employed in the mill itself. Girl apprentices were often obtained from London workhouses. In 1847, Oake Woods opened their bacon factory. The railway arrived in 1859, closely followed by the Gillingham Pottery, Brick and Tile Co. in 1865. A cattle and stock market developed and this was followed by the emergence of firms still existing today, i.e., Bracher Bros, J.H. Rose & Sons, Hudson & Martin, Lights and Sticklands. The population grew from 1,873 in 1801 to 3,380 in 1901.

During the first three decades of the twentieth century, the prosperity of the town continued. A market was held every other Monday and the calf market was the second largest in the country. There was a large dairy depot for manufacturing cheese and supplying milk to London, as well as Eden Shute's butter factory and Slade's mineral works. There was also the smell of Maloney's glue factory! After 1945 there was a steady decline and the end of the market in the 1950s seemed to mark the end of industrial Gillingham.

However, by the 1970s, the trend was reversing and new firms – such as Sherman Chemicals, Biokil, Sigma Aldrich, Wessex Fare, and Chester Jefferies – came to the town. Land was released for housing development and the town started to grow again, sadly without a reasonable infrastructure. However, the 'Relief Road' appeared in the late 1980s, following much controversy and disruption for traders. Le Neubourg Way (named after Gillingham's twin town in Normandy) provided the opportunity for a supermarket to be built. Reputed to be the third busiest Waitrose store in the country, it is now the focal point for the regeneration of the town's retail trade.

In the last ten years, the expansion of Gillingham has also included a huge building and refurbishment programme at the primary schools in School Road and at Milton and also Gillingham School (after the demolition of the old Grammar school). A new primary school was built at Wyke and the town has a new library and museum at Chantry Fields. The quality of education provided in the town has often been the driving force for families moving into the area, such that there is now serious discussion about building another primary school to meet the needs of the new population.

One thing is certain, Gillingham will continue to change and hopefully someone will continue to record those changes.

I hope you enjoy the book!

David Lloyd
1998

One

Around the Town

Chantry Bridge, Gillingham.

Chantry Bridge, 1950. This old footpath over the River Stour leads to Chantry Fields which, until 1993, was the only way to get to the two cottages beyond.

The Square from St Mary's church tower, 1966. Chantry Fields, at the top, is now the site of Waitrose and Le Neubourg Way.

The Square, c. 1911. Slade & Sons dominates this scene. W.E. Samways is the pharmacist and also the photographer for many of the different postcard scenes of the town at this time. The door to the left of Samways' shopfront is the entrance to the post office.

Slade and Sons, c. 1911. This department store opened in 1901. From left to right: Mary Slade, -?-, -?-, Bill Slade Snr, ? Bailey, Hubert Hillier, Bill Slade Jnr, -?-, Arthur Belgin.

High Street, 1960. The Grosvenor Arms' inn buildings, to the left, were demolished in 1996. The trees were part of The Vicarage's garden (now Rawson Court). The car park was built on land in the garden that was purchased by the council.

"The Mill", Gillingham.

The Mill, 1922. The building on the far left, in the process of demolition, was the silk workrooms with the upper dormitory floor used to house the girl apprentices. To the right of it is the silk mill, where the silk was separated from the cocoons. The next part of the building was the grist mill, for the grinding of corn and wheat. The mill manager lived in the house to the right – which still survives. The mill, left derelict for several years, was finally destroyed by fire in 1982. The old waterwheel was bought by the owner of Waterloo Mill at Silton and now awaits restoration.

The Old Bridge Gillingham

The Town Bridge, late 1930s. This is the bridge that John Constable painted in 1823 (the original painting now hangs in the Tate Gallery). The Regal Cinema, on the left, opened in 1934.

J. HERRIDGE & Co.,

WHOLESALE & RETAIL

TEA DEALERS, GROCERS and PROVISION FACTORS.

Ironmongers & General House Furnishers.

GILLINGHAM.

Right: J Herridge & Co., 1906. This was situated opposite Lloyds Bank where ShoeRack and Chantry TV are today.

Below: High Street, *c.* 1904. The building on the right was built from local brick for the Wilts & Dorset Bank in 1877. The bank's roots in the town go back to 1836, when Edward Neave was appointed agent. It was extended in the 1920s and, in 1941, was absorbed by Lloyds Bank.

Bowles' outfitters and hatters, High Street, c. 1911. From the 1920s until the late 1950s, this was Peach's tobacconists and hairdressers. It is now Gylla Galore.

A visit to the town in pony and trap, c. 1916. The children are Joan Lewis (back), Ann Hannam, Betty New and John Lewis. The Wilts & Dorset Bank (now Lloyds) is to the left in the background. The small gate led to 'Fernbank'.

High Street from the bottom of School Road, 1960. Parents congregate to meet their children from school. Mrs Robinson is in the car.

Stickland's ironmongers (on the left), 1920s. The business was started in 1882 by Edwin Roberts Stickland and was continued, until quite recently, by his great-grandson, Peter Crocker. The house to the far left was once owned by James Dunn, a seedsman, whose son later made his family a household name with Dunn's Seeds Ltd.

37474. High Street, Gillingham.

JAMES WEARE,

. . *Baker & Confectioner.*

Pastry, Cakes, Biscuits and Pure Confectionery in great variety and of the best quality.

Turog, Malt, Wholemeal and Milk Bread.

The Machine Bakery,
. . GILLINGHAM.

Above: Junction of High Street, Newbury Road and Station Road, 1906. Stickland's are selling Shell petrol. The shop on the left is Strange's shoe shop.

Left: James Weare, baker and confectioner of Newbury, 1906. He also dispensed homeopathic medicines and kept a temperance hotel.

Right: Peach's saloon, on the site now occupied by Light's garage, 1907. Mr Peach moved to the High Street in the 1920s.

Below: Newbury, 1960. Mr Taplin was a chemist here for many years.

60029. Newbury, Gillingham, Dorset.

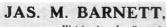

JAS. M. BARNETT,

Watchmaker, Jeweller and Optician,

Invites your inspection of his New and Up-to-date Stock of . .

Wedding and Birthday Presents in great variety.

Also a large Stock of

Engagement, Wedding and Dress Rings, to select from

PERSONAL ATTENTION GIVEN TO REPAIRS.

Spectacles and Eye-Glasses Scientifically Adapted.
Old Gold and Silver Bought or Exchanged.

Newbury St., GILLINGHAM.

Left: Jas M. Barnett, watchmaker, jeweller and optician of Newbury, 1906.

Below: Light's garage, Newbury, 1950s. This was the first garage in Gillingham to have a pull-in forecourt. Motorcycles were sold from the shop on the left. In the buildings behind the tanker was Stone's greengrocery, followed by Bob Pester (prior to his move to Queen Street). The capacity of the tanker shown is half that of modern day vehicles. Regent petrol was sold from 1949 until 1969, when it was taken over by Texaco.

Royal Hotel, Newbury, c. 1920. The garden to the left is now part of Bracher Bros.

Newbury on Market Day, 1904. Bracher Bros, established in 1866, moved to the middle building in 1896. They advertised themselves as cabinetmakers, house furnishers, decorators, painters, paperhangers, upholsterers and undertakers. Note the two lions on the front of the Royal – where's the missing one now?

Mrs George Jukes outside her cottage at Lodden, 1940s.

Duncliffe View, Gillingham

Duncliffe Wood today is one of the largest woods in North Dorset, sitting on the top of Duncliffe Hill, which looks across the Blackmore Vale and the Stour Valley towards Shaftesbury. The hill has probably been clothed in woodland since the retreat of the last ice sheet from Britain over 12,000 years ago. Past owners were King's College and the Forestry Commission. It was acquired by the Woodland Trust in 1985.

Police station and courthouse, School Road, c. 1905. It was built in 1890.

The fire station at the top of School Lane, 1935. This photograph shows brigade members with their Lincoln fire engine. From left to right, back row: J Hine, T. Hayden, T. Flower, A. Sheppard, A. Belgin. Centre row: E. Hine (driver), T. Hillier, J. Webber, H. Luffman, D. Tucker. Front row: H. Harris (captain), J. Burtt, J. Case, L. Brown.

Westminster Bank, 1925. The town's lecture hall was originally on this site but was demolished in 1900 to make way for the new bank premises of Messrs Stuckey & Co. The design was by G.H. Oakley, a Bristol architect. Construction costs were £4,449 (exclusive of sinking a well and providing office fittings). For a short while it was taken over by Parrs, until 1923, when it became the Westminster Bank. In 1970 this organisation merged with the National Provincial to become the National Westminster.

Interior of Westminster Bank, c. 1960. The manager at this time was Mr Shipp. Only half of the ground floor was used as office space. The remainder and upper floors were occupied by the incumbent manager.

Post office, Station Road, 1930s. Miss Lovelace is accompanied by Jack King and Charlie Stickland. Nicholsons, the printers, are to the right.

Station Road, c. 1915. The building to the left, formerly Miss Dunn's High School for girls, was being used at this time by the Red Cross. Indeed, it functioned as a hospital for the duration of the First World War. Afterwards, it became the National Provincial Bank and is now a Masonic lodge.

F. P. COLLIHOLE

General Draper, Milliner, Hosier, &c.

Specialities—
Millinery, Dressmaking, Household Linen, Ladies' Underclothing.

Station Rd., GILLINGHAM.

Left: F.P. Collihole, general draper in Station Road, 1906. These premises were later occupied by Ayles and Owen.

Below: South Western Hotel, 1906. The proprietor at this time was George Bignal, who was to be the grandfather of Mary Bignal-Rand, the Olympic athlete. The hotel was used by commercial travellers that had arrived by rail. On market days, farmers and dealers parked their carts and carriages and hotel staff looked after the horses.

24

Brickyard, late 1960s. The Gillingham Pottery, Brick and Tile Co. was founded in 1865. The first two shareholders were John Williams Bell and Robert Sadler Freame, solicitors who played a major part in the future development of the town. The products of the brickyard were durable and of very good quality – as evidenced by many buildings in the locality. Pipes were made for agricultural drainage and such roof tiles are seen all over the South, in particular Bournemouth. The yard closed in 1968, when production became unprofitable.

Lime Tree House and The Barton, 1966. The Barton was occupied by Shephard Bros, tailors, for many years.

Queen Street from the church tower, 1966.

P. Stacey and Son, Queen Street, 1952. The board on the left advertises the programme for the Regal Cinema and the shop is decorated in preparation for the Queen's visit. Percy Stacey took over the hairdressers from Mr Cole in January 1948 and continued running the business until his death in 1970. His son, Ron, took over until 1984. The shop, next to The Smouldering Boulder, is now a private residence.

The Bay Store, c. 1905. Robert Lush was the proprietor. The field was common land in front of Lodbourne Farmhouse and was used by visiting funfairs and circuses until the early 1960s, when Lodbourne Green was built.

Peacemarsh Stores, late 1960s. This establishment was run by the Smith sisters.

Plank House and Wyke Street, 1960s. The house was used as a hospital during the First World War.

Wyke Road and Beehive cottage, 1930s. The cottage was demolished to make access to the new housing development via Coldharbour. Broad Robin field is to the right.

Marleaze, on the left, and Wyke Road, 1941. Lt Col. Charles Wallis lived in Wyke House (hidden by the trees on the far right). When the Local History Society was formed, in 1953, Col. Wallis was appointed honorary curator and was the driving force behind the society obtaining a museum, an ambition which was achieved in 1958. He was also the brother of Barnes Wallis, the famous inventor.

Wyke Road and maltsters' cottages, 1920s. Matthews' brewery is in the distance.

Wyke Hall, 1930s. Now restored and divided into flats, it was built by Richard de Wyke in the reign of Edward III and still has a minstrel gallery, oak panelling and some parts of the Tudor building. Before the Reformation it was, for a time, supposed to have been a monastery and the lake was presumably the monks' fish pond. During the Second World War, it was used to billet army doctors and nursing sisters.

Thorngrove House, Common Mead Lane, 1966. This Victorian house was once owned by Sir Harold and Lady Pelly. It was used during the Second World War as a billet for American officers and, afterwards, as a Dr Barnardo's childrens' home. Today, it is owned by Scope and is part of a horticultural work centre.

The Viaduct, 1920s. This is situated where the London to Exeter railway line crosses the Kington Magna road. Edgar Samways took this photograph.

Rolls Bridge. Gillingham.

Rolls Bridge Farm, 1929. All the fields of the farm are now developed for housing and only one of the original farm buildings remain.

General view of Gillingham, taken in 1929.

Two

Gillingham at Work

Workmen at Maloneys, Station Road, *c.* 1920.

Above: Saddlery at Newbury, *c.* 1900. Mr George Gibbs Conway is the saddler and harness maker. The building is just to the right of the footpath down to the railway platform. Mr Read, and then Mr Ozzard – a tinsmith, occupied the site for many years after this photograph was taken.

Left: 'Jack' Ozzard of Newbury. Jack's father, William, ran his business from 1914, initially in Railway Terrace and then on Railway Bridge.

Right: Len Fudge working with his lathe at the Rotary Works in Station Road, 1920s. The Lion Engine Co. was one of many enterprises run by Charlie Maloney and produced small engines, which were used by farmers nationally as well as in developing countries. One surviving example of these engines can be seen in the Museum.

Below: Three generations of the Ozzard family – Jack, William and Roy – at their workshop in Newbury, 1950s.

Left: Milmer Brown, postman, 1900. He was also verger at St Mary's church for forty-four years.

Below: Harry Case, c. 1920. The tins of biscuits were supplied by McVitie & Price and W. & R. Jacob & Company.

Hudson & Martin staff at the sawmills in Station Road, 1924. This was on the site now occupied by Sherman Chemicals. The sawmills closed in 1960.

Oil Agency staff at the brickyard depot, late 1950s. From left to right: Billy Dennett, Bill Andrews, ? White, Mickey Martin, -?-, Jim ?, Harry Hunt.

Harry Allard and his pigs at Lodden Farm, 1920s. Harry's children in the background are, from left to right: Bert, Joe and Jack.

Farmer Pitman at Culvers. His son, Vic, is on the back of the tractor and the children are probably from the Collis family.

Sawing wood at Springfield, Bugley, 1915. This was owned by the Hannam family at this time.

Mr A. Francis controls the horses at harvest time, Cole Street Farm, late 1940s.

Bob Pester, greengrocer, 1956. He was well known in the area from his grocery round and he is pictured here in Fairey Crescent with Joan Dear and her children: Terry, Raymond and Rosalyn.

Geoff Kite on deliveries. He and his family were fishmongers in the town for many years with a shop in the High Street, which is now occupied by the Abbey Friar.

Right: Fred Proudley, hardware merchant. The business was started in the late 1920s by Fred's father, John, in the Old Forge at Peacemarsh.

Below: Proudley's van, late 1950s. Fred's son, Eric, still continues a van service today in Gillingham and the surrounding villages.

London Central Meat Co., near the church gate, High Street, 1935. The site is now occupied by 'Scenes'.

Miss Smith serves Barry Young at Peacemarsh Stores, c. 1967.

Oake Woods, Station Road, 1963. T.A. James, the manager (right), and the sales manager, Jack Stone, discuss sales matters as a van is being loaded at the factory.

The Wiltshire cutting line at Oake Woods, 1963. On the left are: Vic Lane, Cecil Coombes, Frank Hutchinson, Taff Pritchard, Bob Vowles, Roger Lydford, Gid Stone. On the right: Stan Randall, Dusty Millard, Bob Smith, Butch Harris (hidden), Art Butt, Gid Stone.

Ballast cleaning on the track just past Railway Terrace, 1966. British Rail staff include Ted Lankey, George Bealing, Cliff Lloyd, Inspector Tolley, Fred Hopkins, Bill Fishley and Mervyn Biss. The machinery was Swiss made and the task involved a twenty-four hour operation on a Sunday.

Tommy Suttle and Nurse Read, The Pharmacy, The Square, late 1960s. Tommy took over from Ernest Samways in 1964 and continued until his retirement in 1988. The shop is now known as St Mary's Pharmacy. Nurse Read was the district nurse and midwife for about thirty years.

Three

Church and Chapel

St Mary's church. The *Domesday Book* records that the church was granted by William the Conqueror to the Abbey of Shaftesbury. The oldest part of the present building is the chancel, built in the Decorated style (1270-1370). The medieval nave was demolished in 1838 and rebuilt by the Revd Henry Deane, vicar of the church from 1832 until 1882.

Interior of St Mary's church, 1905. The galleries, upper left and right, were removed in 1918. This reduced the seating capacity but the added light and improved appearance of the church more than compensated for this loss.

The Vicarage, Queen Street, 1907. This building dates from 1883, but there has been a residence for the incumbent on this same site from the institution of the first vicar in 1318. In the time of Canon John Fisher, the painter John Constable (1770–1837), his friend, was a visitor. From 1916, the curates were expected to live in The Vicarage.

Bird's eye view of The Vicarage and gardens, 1966. The garden once extended to the river, with the lower part used for vegetable growing (now the car park) and the upper part utilized for the annual church fête. Both the building and the garden are now incorporated into Rawson Court.

Nativity scene in St Mary's church, c. 1950. From left to right are: Michael Rose, Susan Raymond, Mary Brickell, Dennis Hannam, Lyn Light, Bob Carter. The identity of the girls kneeling down is uncertain.

Sister Hart and her Bible class, photographed in the playground of the original Wyke School, 1944. From left to right, back row: Margaret Cox, Brenda Scammell, Dorothy Gray, Alwyn Case, Kitty Perrot, Eileen Cross, Joyce King, Pat Francis. Front row: Ruth Martin and Sister Hart.

Interior of the Catholic church, Cemetery Road, c. 1925. The church was converted from two cottages given by the Freame family and dedicated to St Benedict. The church was destroyed by fire in September 1929 and was rebuilt, and then later enlarged, in 1952 and 1976.

Primitive Methodist church, Queen Street. This was built in 1876 to replace the original 1836 church in Turners Lane (now a private residence). The Queen Street Society, as they became known, operated independently to the High Street Weslyans until 1963, when the Queen Street church was closed. It was subsequently taken over by the Royal Yachting Association, which had links in the town for many years, and is now owned and used by 'Materialize'.

Revd F. Adams outside the old Baptist church, Newbury, 1950s. The building was demolished in 1970.

Helpers at the Methodist church. Ruth Welch, Kath Rose, -?-, Kath Rawlins, -?-, Doris Welch, -?-, Addie Bracher, -?-.

Methodist Sunday School. On the far left are Doris Welch and Joyce Drewitt.

Four

View of the Villages

Milton on Stour, 1930s. The blacksmith's house is facing the camera and the forge was on the other side. Freddie Vincent, the blacksmith, made the porch to the adjoining house on the left. This was where Samuel Braddick once lived before he moved into Station Road.

Bob England's store and post office at Milton, late 1930s.

The Kendalls, Milton. This was the home of Blandford and Ina Matthews (of GB Matthews' brewery) in the 1970s.

Spicketts Farmhouse opposite Milton church, 1950s. The house is 200 years old and was formerly held by the Matthews family. For the past 100 years it has been occupied by three generations of the Knapton family. Unusual features of the building include the wrought-iron verandahs and the inwardly-opening windows.

East Stour vehicle specially adapted by Mr Budden for use by the Air Raid Wardens during the Second World War.

Arthur Farthing, engineer at Hindleys', Bourton, 1915. Arthur travelled the whole country on behalf of the company and this photograph was used on publicity material.

Hindleys' workshop, c. 1915. This is part of the erecting shops for the high-speed gas engines.

Right: Waterwheel at Hindleys' works. Built in 1837, this wheel was reputed to be the largest in England.

Below: Workers at Hindleys' Bourton foundry.

BOURTON FOUNDRY

Above: The Elsworth twins on the shell case, 1930s. This was on the triangle of green (now gone) at West Stour, a popular place for children to play or take car numbers. The girls are facing the road to the church and the A30 runs behind them.

Left: The Trim family of West Stour, 1900. Eden Trim with children Charlie, May and Roland. The photograph was taken by Charles Johnson of Gillingham.

The Burgess family at West Stour, c. 1900. From left to right: Charles, George, Mr Burgess, Margaret, Olive, Mrs Burgess, Sid and Lucy.

Sunday School gathering at West Stour, c. 1900. The medals were given for regular attendance and good conduct.

Farmworkers at Manor Farm, West Stour, 1911. From left to right: Mr Burgess, Walter Lloyd and George Wetherall.

West Stour School group with teacher Mrs Gray, c. 1920. Fourth from the left in the back row is Miss Gibbs (infant teacher), whilst on her left is Vida Lloyd. From left to right, front row: -?-, ? Cox, Christina Lloyd, ? Gray, ? Gray, ? Flower and Harold Cox (who later married Christina)

Right: Harry Lloyd at West Stour, 1911. The brass head of the ceremonial stave is decorated with a ship design, probably linked to the Ship Inn, and was used on special occasions of the East and West Stour and Fifehead Magdalen Club (founded in 1762). Harry was well known in the village for his garland making and leading the club's walks.

Below: Coronation celebrations at West Stour, 1911. The Ship Inn is in the background. The marquee was supplied by Hudson & Martin of Gillingham and Harry Lloyd is holding his stave and garland in the back row.

Mr Wetherall at Highbridge Mill, East Stour, c. 1920. The vehicle on the left was registered in the name of William Wetherall and is described in registration records as a black, twenty-horsepower, one ton truck.

Highbridge Mill, East Stour. Powered by the River Stour, the mill ground locally-grown barley and wheat into flour for pigs. It went out of use at the beginning of the twentieth century.

East Stour Home Guard, 1940s.

The Stours Orchestra, 1930s. This organisation was founded in East Stour by C.E. Davies, a former London orchestra musician. From left to right, back row: Sidney Compton, Joe Fowles, George Harris, Walter Morgan. Middle row: Fred Fowles, ? Brickell, A. Maidment, C.E. Davies, Dan Tucker, Taylor Jones, G. Fowles, Charlie Marvin. Front row: Mrs Davies, Celia Fowles, Mrs H. Butler, Mrs Dick Veal, Charlie Raymond, Wilfred Gibbons.

The Vicarage, Fifehead Magdalen. This building was described in the Historical Monuments survey (of 1972) as having two storeys, rubble walls – in part rendered, with ashlar dressings – and a thatched roof. It is probably of seventeenth-century origin with eighteenth-century alterations and enlargement. It is now a private residence.

Fifehead House, Fifehead Magdalen. Demolished in 1964, it possessed three storeys, with ashlar walls and slate-covered roofs. It was built in 1807 to replace the Tudor manor that stood there.

Threshing at Middle Farm, Fifehead Magdalen, 1941.

Carpenters' workshop at Stour Row in 1903. The workers are, from left to right (probably): James Kiddle, Bill Hull, Bert Pike, Jimmy Pike and Jimmy Pike Snr.

Cockerell's bakery and shop, Kington Magna, c. 1911.

Kington Magna School group, 1954/55. From left to right: John Highnam, Donald Hinks, Nigel Dyke, Robert Counsell, Robin Draycott, Stan Chard, Pat Osborne, David Evans (headmaster). Middle row: Douglas Dyke, Nicholas Hopkins, Philip Arnold, David Draycott, Malcolm Bullen, Christopher Mason, Gerald Hinks. Front row: Susan Tutcher, Brenda Wareham, Yvonne Higgins, Beverly Evans, Angela Tutcher, Pauline Bennett.

Right: Charlie Ash and Keith Richards take a break from their groom duties at the National Stud, Sandley, October 1964. One month later, the Stud moved its headquarters to Newmarket.

Below: Kington Magna and Buckhorn Weston Home Guard, *c.* 1942. From left to right, back row: Ernie Hibbs, Cecil Crew, Claude Sennick, Eric Dowding, Stan Cox, Phil Perrett, Arthur Beale. Middle row: Burnice Lewis, -?-, -?-, Len Dowding, George Dowding, -?-, -?-, -?-. Front row: Harry Wareham, -?-, Arthur Arnold, Bert Foyle, Les Cockerell, Percy Cox, Bert Cox Jnr, Percy Newport

The family of Thomas and Edith Arnold and their six children (and Benny the dog) at Bowden, Kington Magna, c. 1926. From left to right, back row: Harry, Bessie (Hallett), Jack, Jim. Front row: Mabel (Kendall), Thomas, Edith (née Hayward), Mary (Lewis).

Kington Magna Women's Institute, 1950s. From left to right, back row: Mrs Irene Arnold, Mrs J. Stokes, Mrs Linda Dowding, Miss Daisy Gillett, Mrs A. Hoskins, Mrs Brenda Evans. Front row: Mrs E. Hayter, Miss Caddy, Mrs P. Cox, Miss P. Reynolds, Mrs S. Wall.

Kington Magna football team and supporters, 1956. From left to right, back row: Mary Feltham, Bert Cox Jnr, Mrs Owen Shaw, Bert Cox Snr, Tom Arnold, Jack Osborne, Tony Osborne, Ron Luffman, Ernie Stokes, Horst Schroeder, Frank Galleymore, Frank Curtis, Jack Watts, Fred Osborne, Revd Frank Edwards, Fred Bateman, -?-, Irene Arnold. Front row: Cecil Crew, Bob Underdown, Geoff Dowding, Dick Arnold, Owen Shaw, Bob Holly, George Baumgarten, Fred Crew, Arthur Arnold. Sitting, cross-legged: George Osborne, Ray Crew.

Kington Magna church choir, mid-1950s. From left to right, back row: Chris Highnam, Bill Reynolds, Tom Arnold, David Evans Jnr, Daisy Gillett, Bertie Read, Evelyn Raymond, Bill Dowding, David Evans Snr, Geoff Dowding, Clarence Dowding. Front row: Philip Arnold, Esme Spenn, Brenda Wareham, Doreen Hanham, Ruth Goodship, Joyce Dowding, Yvonne Higgins, Dianne Arnold, Doreen Drake.

Milkers at Manor Farm, Silton. These workers would have used traditional hand-milking methods.

A milker at Manor Farm with his 'modern' equipment.

Former pupils at the centenary celebrations of Woodville School, Stour Provost. A boarding school (mixed) with a residence for a master was built in 1850. From left to right, back row: John Cox, Mrs Edith Farthing, Arthur Maidment, Mrs Mabel Lloyd. Front row: Mrs Lockyer, Mrs Alice Martin, Charlie Pike, Mrs Ralph. Edith Farthing (née Beale) is recorded in the school's records of June 1894 as being away ill 'with inflammation of lung hardly expected to pull through it'.

Milk delivery, c. 1910. The name on the cart is George Fricker, of Huntingford.

Blackmore Vale Hunt at the Stapleton Arms, Buckhorn Weston

Empire Day at Buckhorn Weston School, *c.* 1903.

Five

Transport

Walter Hunt with two of P.O. Baker's Model-T cars, 1920s. Baker's started in business in 1912.

Left: Mrs Agnes Bell, as photographed by Adam Gosney of Sherborne, c. 1882. Mrs Bell, the mother of John Williams Bell, solicitor, died 4 September 1886, aged ninety-four years. She was obviously a well-respected person as, on her funeral day, nearly all the houses were veiled and the shops closed from Knapp House to the church. The bier was preceded by the gentlemen of the town, with most of the leading tradesmen following behind.

Below: Mabel Beale with her bicycle, 1902. Magnet bicycles, such as this one, were manufactured in Gillingham by Light's of Newbury. W. Phillips of East Stour took this photograph.

E.J. Wiles' horse and van, c. 1930. The bakery was in Hardings Lane.

W.E. Butler's railway delivery wagon.

Sidney Hannam with his four-horsepower BSA and sidecar, c. 1920. This was purchased from E.R. Stickland of Gillingham. The passengers are daughters, Ann and Martha.

Sid Kite on deliveries, 1910. William Kite was fishmonger, fruiterer and licensed dealer in game.

Wiles, coal merchants, operated from Peacemarsh and the station yard in the 1950s. Mr Hardcastle and Mr Chandler were the coalmen.

Michael Rose with Braddicks' lorry and tractor, 1952. The tractor was being collected from Doncaster to be supplied to Gordon Pickford of Stourton.

Matthews and Co. Austin lorry, c. 1950. The Matthews family operated from their brewery in Wyke for about 200 years, until they sold out to Hall and Woodhouse in 1963. The brewery used a buffalo as a trade mark.

Ruth Welch and Jean Ayles of Hunt's Dairies, New Road, 1960s.

S. Braddick & Son, Station Road, 1950s. Samuel Braddick originally started up in business as a blacksmith at Milton. When he started dealing in farm machinery, in 1917, he moved to Station Road. The buildings shown are now fronted by the Rover garage.

J.H. Rose & Sons's Austin lorry, 1956. The firm was started by John Henry Rose in 1889, with a borrowed horse and cart, and hauled coal from Radstock. By its centenary year, the firm employed twenty staff, ran around twenty vehicles and could boast a turnover of £1,000,000.

Above: Battle of Britain AA Command engine 34049 prepares to pull a train loaded with horses. This was a result of the National Stud transferring from Sandley to Newmarket in 1964. The boxes came from all over the Southwest and it took a week to establish the train.

Left: Issetta bubble car made by BMW and owned by Phil Bland, local insurance agent, pictured here with his daughter, Carola, in 1962.

Six

Wartime Gillingham

Milmer Brown, the church verger, looks on as Mr Toogood and Sid Court remove the railings for the war effort. Mrs Court ran a scrapyard at Kingscourt.

Left: Mr Jukes proudly displays his uniform at his house in Lodden during the First World War.

Below: Women's Volunteer Service canteen workers, Second World War. The group includes: Mrs Thorne, Mrs Perrett, Mrs Hurley, Mrs Stocker, Mrs White, Mrs Stevens and Mrs Coward.

Right: Mrs Court at Kingscourt during the Second World War. Apart from dealing in scrap, she was obviously in the market for other commodities – but no luck on this occasion!

Below: Royal Observer Corps, Second World War. From left to right, back row: A. Allard, C. White, R. Wadman. Middle row: H. Wiles, J. Herridge, M. Roberts, G. Jaggard, W. Tooze, G. Stone. Front row: H. Martin, ? Jukes, J. Scammell, E. Jukes. A post was set up near the football field and manned throughout the war, plotting all the German formations that raided Bristol.

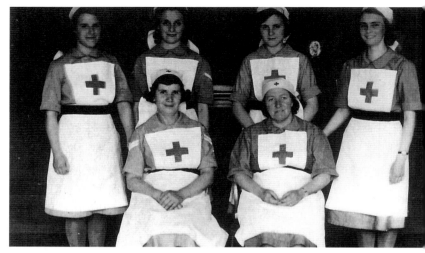

Red Cross group at the end of the Second World War. From left to right, back row: Eileen Cross, Joan Burt, Yvonne Ringh, Sheila Coombes. Front row: Rita Palmer, Mrs Victor Wadman.

Civil Defence first aid post at Newbury, Second World War. From left to right, back row: -?-, S. Strange, ? Coombes, C. Dicker. Middle row: Mrs Wadman, Hilda Collier, Mrs Scovell, Mrs Doris Johnston, -?- (evacuee), Miss Down, Mrs Edwards, Mrs Deam, Miss Bishop, Mrs Beaton, Miss Coombes, Mrs Jaggard, Mrs Molly Griffiths. Front row: Joan Walters (evacuee), Mrs Freda Howe, Miss B. Bracher, Mrs Buckley, Ivy Hiscock, Dorothy Brickell, Mrs Dickenson.

Right: Private Lloyd CW 5726668, 4th Battalion, Dorset Regiment, 43 Wessex Division, 1940. Cliff and many of the local lads were members of the volunteer Territorial (or 4th Battalion). Called up at the outbreak of the Second World War, most of the war years were spent in coastal areas of Britain. In 1944, the 4th Battalion were involved in Operation Market Garden in Holland. This was a complex and daring attempt to capture the river crossings near Arnhem to cover the evacuation of the 1st Airborne. Under constant enemy fire, only 300 Dorsets survived the crossing, but 2,400 paratroopers were ferried back. Although Cliff survived, he was captured and spent the remainder of the war as a POW.

Below: Threshing gang, 1941. R. Pitman and L. Trim with the Land Girls evacuated from Barrett's sweet factory in London.

Left: Charles Brown, RAMC, 1941. By December 1940, there were three General Hospital Units in Gillingham (numbers 37, 55 and 56). All of these went out to West Africa during May and June of 1941. Doctors and medical officers were billeted in the Lodbourne area and the nursing sisters at Wyke Hall.

Below: Air Training Corp 932 Flight at the grammar school, 1940. From left to right, back row: -?-, ? Taylor, R. Cullingford, -?-, J. Garrett, A. Jukes, D. Chislett, P. White, J. Bracher, P. Flower, D. King, J. Gale, K. Stokes, W. Burchell. Middle row: L. Tanswell, D. Waring, P. West, -?-, D. Lawley, -?-, J. Morgan, J. Case, -?-, H. Mathias, E. Hunt, A. Taylor, R. Taylor, R. Lydford. Front row: P. Gale, A. Southgate, S. Ford, P. Webber, ? Ford, C. Ford, C. Howe, R.V. Best, F/Lt Hurley, G. Guard, R. Whitmarsh, L. Hooper, R. Gray, T. Arnold, P. Steele, D. Hanham. Seated: -?-, B. Stokes, -?-, ? Lawrence, P. Bland, C. Read, E. Sage, K. Harcourt, R. Doggrell, J. Heal.

Right: Sgt C.W. Brooks 31352268 of Company 'A', 277th Combat Engineer Battalion, US Army. Sgt Brooks was one of many American soldiers who camped in Gillingham during 1944, prior to the D-Day landings in France.

Below: Royal Army Medical Corps vehicle, 1941. The RAMC used Gillingham as a mobilising centre and, although the size of the units is uncertain, most were usually equipped and staffed to run 600 beds and had around sixteen medical officers and fifty nursing sisters.

Left: Mr Albert Harrison, ARP warden, 1940s. Mr Harrison was the manager of the Co-op store in Queen Street from 1919 until the mid-1950s. He was on various committees and was treasurer of the town band for twenty-five years.

Below: ATC group at *HMS Dipper*, Henstridge Aerodrome, c. 1942. The plane in the background is a Seafire, the naval version of the Spitfire. From left to right, back row: Mervyn Biss, Ted Hunt, A. Arnold, M. Cross, Ken Dukes, ? Smith, M. Davis, Ivor Scammell. Third row: Ian Nicholson, R. Galbally, John Light, Norman Brickell, Ken Jukes, ? Avery, Stan Hine, C. Palmer. Second row: ? Snook, Ken Taylor, Ted Hardy, A. Lawrence, A. Fry, J. Fulcher, Ron Bristow, John Burgess. Front row: Phil Francis, S. Ford, P. White, RNAS Officer, W. Hurley (Commanding Officer), Brian Hurley, Ray Lydford, Laurie Hull, P. Gale.

Seven

Schooldays

GILLINGHAM.

A NATIONAL SCHOOL for Girls and Boys, will be shortly opened at the new School Room, near the Vicarage.

All the children will be taught reading, writing, summing, and knitting; and the girls will be taught needle-work.

Each child will pay one penny a week.

No child can be admitted under six years old; nor any who does not know the alphabet.

Parents wishing to send their children to this School, are requested to call at the Vicarage any morning between eight and ten o'clock.

August, 1839.

Neave, Printer, Gillingham.

National School notice, as distributed by Revd Henry Deane, vicar of St Mary's.

St Martin's Priory School in Queen Street, 1933.

County Primary School in School Road. Opened in 1875 and known as the Board School, it had an infant section and separate sections for boys and girls. This photograph was taken on 8 May 1977. Some days later, the buildings to the left and centre were devastated by fire. The school was rebuilt and the building on the right was retained and, in 1997, extended and incorporated into yet another new building as part of a major re-development scheme to cater for Gillingham's growing school population.

Class at County Primary School, late 1920s. From left to right, back row: ? Stone, Hilda Harrison, Miss Burt, Joan Coward, Jessica Hussey, Arthur Read. Second row: Joyce Rideout, Ivy Hiscock, Cyril Rowsell, Beryl Luffman, Len King. Third row: Ethel Hiscock, Molly Goodsen, Joan Flower, Mabel Miles, Phil Read. Front row: Eric Mansfield, Harry Whatley, Claude Street, Jack Read, Alice Thick.

County Primary choir, 1935. From left to right, back row: Marion Batts, Elsie Alner, Vera Gray, Mabel Miles, Gwen Stone, Ivy Hiscock. Middle row: Alice Thick, Joan Coward, Joan Flower, Myrtle Green, Joyce Burden, Jessica Hussey, Joyce Ridout, Kathleen Warr, Marjorie Setter, Beryl Luffman, Winnie Burden, Dorothy Kingham. Front row: -?-, -?-, Dorothy Welstead, Miss Stiling, Eileen Larcombe, Margaret Mansfield, -?- .

Mr Alfred Knott and the County Primary football team, 1935. From left to right: Mr Knott (trainer), R. Light, L. Gatehouse, R. White, A. Bullen, R. Harris, W. Andrew (manager). Front row: A. Read, C. Street, Cecil Collis, Percy Alger and Ron Hussey. Mr Locke was the headmaster at this time and Mr Knott and Mr Andrews were the only teachers at the school.

County Primary, c. 1950. Miss Jean Walker (who later married George Joyce) takes advantage of good weather to hold her class in the playground. The pupils are, from left to right: -?-, -?-, Chris Harding, Keith Francis, -?-, Robin Sadler, Peter Trowbridge, Janette Bird, Rosemary Hardcastle and Maureen Gatehouse. In the background, to the left, is Murial Allard's car.

County Primary class of 1959. From left to right, back row: Richard Gwilt, Robin Chard, Richard Lush, -?-, John Green, Roger Chant, Peter Cornford, Alan Whitehead, -?-, Peter Collis. Middle row: -?-, Elizabeth Higgin, Moira Green, Susan Bland, Noelle Francis, Elizabeth Stainer, Sally Trainor, Janice Hinson, Christine Coward, Nicola Hughes, Beryl Bashford, Christine Cadman. Front row: Christine Hatch, Beatrice Conway, Olivia Green, Cathy Kite, Sue Perry, Jane Greenstock, -?-, Ann Evans, Marion Bridle, Jill Gray, Angela Maidment, Linda Read.

Mr Dowse and the football team at County Primary, 1957. From left to right, back row: Ken Hardcastle, Richard Watts, Malcolm Jaggard, Mr Dowse, Bernard Gatehouse, David Ayles, Geoff Peters. Front row: Roy Palmer, Ian Maidment, John Betteridge, Roger Griffiths, Ian McQueen, Tim Suter.

Carey Camp, Wareham, 1959. This facility is still used by schools today, but is now known as the Carey Outdoor Education Centre. From left to right, back row: Miss Corbin, Michael Hicks, David Brewer, Graham Hughes, Michael Chant, David Brown, Roy Whitehead, Andrew Dunn, David Lloyd, Graham Hacker, Mr Trickett (headteacher). Front row: A.Yeatman, Sheila Davison, Carol Read, Ann Jaggard, Anne Denslow, Jackie Rice, Nesta Legg, Carol Sheppard, Shirley Flower, Mary Bridle, ? Cross, ? Yeatman, Erika Bland.

Mr Gwilt's class at County Primary School, 1967. From left to right, back row: Paul Luffman, Keith Manning, Douglas Knox, Keith Weeks, Geoffrey Yeatman, Simon Gay, Colin Gay. Middle row: Tony Sorrell, John Hodgson, Robert Koch, Jane Newcombe, Lyn Sorrell, Pam Philips, Dereck King, Lawrence Green, Rodney Drewitt. Front row: Amanda Biss, Rachel Suttle, Anette Ivy, Penny Abbot, Isla Palmer, Susan Lowry, Claire Luffman, Margret Philips, Hilary Birchall, Anita Scott.

Secondary Modern School, 1951. Built just before the Second World War, near to the Grammar School, the new school was at first occupied by pupils from the local primary school, to prevent the building being used as army billets. After the war, comprehensive education was discussed and argued for many years until finally, in 1959, the Secondary Modern and Grammar Schools merged. The buildings now form part of the newly extended and refurbished Gillingham School.

Secondary Modern School class, c. 1950. From left to right, back row: J. Osbourne, D. Curtis, D. Topp, M. Jones, I. Perry, P. Curtis, T. Cull, D. Hunt, D. Burton, J. Perrin. Third row: P. Hillier, ? Hanham, D. Gray, ? Boswell, M. Pike, R. Barter, P. Baumber, T. Harris, R. Bird, P. Dawe. Second row: D. Collis, P. Perrot, J. Stokes, J. Ralph, R. White, J. Ralph, D. Stone. Front row: G. Parsons, P. Target, J. Chalke, R. Frampton, P. Clarke, D. Adams, B. Mead, P. Thompson.

Grammar School, 1894. Founded in 1516 and known as The Free School until the new Gillingham Grammar School was officially opened in 1876.

Grammar School cricket team, 1894.

Grammar School prefects, 1894.

Typical Grammar School classroom at the turn of the twentieth century.

Swimming in the River Shreen at Bay, 1894. This was a popular spot for all local children, being shallow and safe to swim in. The school acquired its own baths in 1912 (off Bay Lane). During excavations for the pool, an ancient gravel bed was revealed and a series of oak posts was found, along with other evidence of a Neolithic lake-dwellers settlement dating from about 2500 BC.

Grammar School football team, 1894.

Bicycle racing on Sports Day at the Secondary Modern School, 1958

Boys from the Secondary Modern School enjoying Swimming Sports Day, 1958. Ken Hardcastle is in the water and Miss Calendar is giving encouragement.

Left: Pat Chamberlain entered the Grammar School in 1941 and is pictured here in her new uniform. She returned to school in 1954 as a member of the teaching staff and eventually became senior mistress and then deputy head in the subsequent comprehensive school. When the governors agreed to admit girls to the school in 1916 they pronounced that '...all girls are required to wear a straw hat and the school hatband'.

Below: Grammar School drive, 1941. The cricket pavilion was built in 1923 by the old boys of the school as a memorial to those of their comrades who had died in the First World War.

Grammar School, Gillingham, (Dorset).

copyright.
G&M. 24.

The last group of Grammar School teachers, Summer 1959. From left to right, back row: Mrs Jaggard (bursar), Mr Griffiths, Mr Evans, Mrs Easterbrook, Miss Westwood, Mr Hartley, Mr Jones, Mrs Esposito, Miss M. Scott, Miss E. Smith, Miss S. Appleby. Front row: Mr Yelling, Mr Hicks, Mr Hurley, Miss Chamberlain, Mr Webster (head), Mr Wagner, Mr Best, Mr Hunt, Mr Elphick.

The Grammar School's production of A Midsummer's Night Dream, December 1954. From left to right, back row: Gillian Ward, John Flashman, Clarence Dowding, Mark Loader, ? Taylor, -?-, David Stone, Margaret Hanham, David Trickett, Tom Vernon (now of *Fat Man on a Bicycle* fame), David Hopkins, Leonard Cowley, Sam Woodcock, Veronica Cowell. Front row: Anne Foulds, Wendy Few, Alan Rogers, Heather Cutler, Walters, Bridget Gantley, Janet Woods, Ivy Cox, June Collins.

Pat Chamberlain presents a retirement gift to Walter Edwin Hurley after a forty-four year long teaching career at Gillingham. He was described as a 'great schoolmaster, scientist and sportsman'. He was also well known for his singing and acting abilities.

Mr Hurley and his wife are guests of honour at a presentation dinner and dance to celebrate his retirement. 180 guests attended, representing the governing body, staff and old boys and girls.

Gillingham School Army Cadet Force, 1964. From left to right, back row: -?-, Mike Hicks, Robert Jordan, Kenny Oliver, David Jeans, David Cooper, Ian Norris. Middle row: Peter Stainer, Steve Guppy, Mike Chant, Bruce Cook, Bob Gristwood. Front row: George Flower, Peter Wells, -?-, Capt. Neil, N. Hawkswell, Nigel Forward, -?-.

Wyke School pupils, 1926. From left to right, back row: Miss Foot, -?-, Mark Fry, -?-, Ron Davies, -?-. Middle row: Herbert Green, ? Gould, Stella Doggrell. Front: -?-, -?-, Joyce Collis, Tom Fry, Roy Green, -?- and Kath Collis. The original school was built in 1890 at the junction of Wyke road and Lydfords Lane.

Miss Margaret Kirkham (deputy head) and Mrs Angela Dawson (teacher) open the gates at the newly-built Wyke Primary School in Deane Avenue for the first seventy-five pupils, 4 September 1991. Baroness Cox, the deputy speaker of the House of Lords, officially opened the school, built to take 210 pupils, on 22 November 1991.

Eight

Life and Leisure

Camping in Chantry Fields, c. 1913. The sign on the tent says 'Back to the Land'. From left to right, back row: -?-, Ted Hiscock, A. Hussey, C. Parfitt, G. Broomfield, T. Foot. Front row: W. Edwards, A. Burton, S. Smith.

Left: Harold Reed relaxing at Oakleigh, Wyke, 1908.

Below: North Dorset election, 1906.

Right: The ornate Edwardian mantelpiece at Oakleigh, Wyke, 1908.

Below: Eliza Stickland seated at the piano with family and friends at Oakleigh, Wyke, 1908

The Lumsden Lambs (members of the Bible class club named after Revd Lumsden) football team. Matches were played in Chantry Fields. From left to right, back row: Billy Edwards, Edgar Green, Gus Broomfield, C. Stickland, ? Harris. Front row: Bert Hiscock, -?-, Percy Lodge, Bill Coward, Stanley Coward.

Territorial football team, 1921/1922 season. The team were winners of the Dorset Team Challenge Cup. From left to right, back row: Cpl A.S. Musselwhite, R. Dukes, S. Bowden, J.R. Algar, Sgt Instr. W.A. Slocombe. Middle row: H.C. Luffman, Sgt W.E. Edwards, W.V. White, H.B. Flower, R. Elcock. Front row: R.H. White, F. Broomfield, H. Francis, T. Marsh, E.P. Hooper.

Town football club, 1938/39 season. From left to right, back row: Charlie Gray, Fred Case, Harry Collarbone, Mr Drake, Mr Beaton, Arthur Shephard, Reg Gray, Bill Miles. Next row (standing): Bert Rose, Jim Maidment, Ken Harris, Roy George, John Harkness. Third row: Eric White, 'Jock' Trainer, George Maidment, Frank Lane. Second row (seated): Bert Collis, Glyn Lawley, Ted Duffett. Front row: George Collis, Ron Frances, Vic Lovell, Fred White.

Town football club, 1966. From left to right, back row: Fred Brown, Maurice Hannam, Derek Martin, Gerald White, Chris Vassie, Dave Parsons, Ken Warren, Tommy Whiffen, 'Dinger' Bell, Mick Osborne, Mr Hine, Terry Lush. Front row: Ray Crew, Brian Flower, Peter Riglar, Len Arney, Gordon Luffman.

Gillingham Agricultural Show, 1913. Herb Gibbs, from Cole Street Farm, with Violet and her foal, winning first prize. Ted Duffett and his family ran the farm.

Gillingham Agricultural Show, 1920s. Harry Dufosee, Harry Allard and Jim Bastable are in the photograph.

Gillingham Agricultural Show, 8 September 1913. These shows were held at Lodden Farm, where the football pitch is today.

Market day in Station Road, 1930s.

The wedding day of Kit Stickland and Charles Reed, pictured at Oakleigh, Wyke, 1909.

Wedding of Reg Budgen to Hilda Martin at Queen Street Methodist church, 1932. From left to right, back row: Phoebe Martin, Rose Martin, Jack Burt (best man), Dollie Martin, Pearl Coward, Hannah Myall, -?-, Reg Martin and Nellie Hiscock with Ken and Doris. Front row: Mr and Mrs Budgen, Ivy Hiscock, Reg Budgen, Hilda Martin, Joyce Martin, Kate Martin, Tom Martin.

Right: Wartime wedding of Fred Martin and his bride, 1942.

Below: Wedding group at the South Western Hotel.

Left: Gondoliers, alias Bill Slade, Arthur Shephard and Eric Nicholson, 1925. This photograph was taken by Ernest Berry.

Below: The Operatic Society in costume for their 1925 production of Gilbert and Sullivan's *The Gondoliers*.

THE GONDOLIERS
Gillingham Operatic Society 1925

Cole's Fair at Gillingham, before the First World War.

Outing to Gough's Caves at Cheddar in Mr Lawley's charabanc, 1920s. Polly and Nellie Dunning are the two passengers at the rear and a young Phil Read is next to the driver's seat.

May Day celebrations in Dr Walker's garden, Newbury, 1941. From left to right, back row: Brenda White, Pam Wadham, Joyce Hooper, Betty Coombs, Sheila Coombs, Janet Stocker, Daphne Bland, Esther Harding, Hazel White, Colleen Raymond, Enid Gray, Pauline ?, Eileen Cross, -?-, Diana Case, Ruth Martin, Joan Luffman. Front row: Freda White, Pam Hillier, Molly Harding.

Blackmore Vale Hunt meeting in The Square.

Gillingham Imperial Silver Band with bandmaster Walt Morgan, 1936.

Tommy Trinder of radio, films and music hall fame takes the baton to the town's band during a special festival week, 20 June 1970. Robert Smith is the player who needs to pay attention!

Children's carnival, 1930.

King George V's Jubilee carnival, 1935. Phil Read holds 'The Gillingham Ox' sign.

Right: Mr Arthur Bell (1891-1976), known affectionately as 'Dinger'. He was a founder member of the carnival when it was revived in the 1950s and loved to lead the procession, on this occasion in the 1960s, mounted on a donkey. After leaving Wyke School, he worked for Frank Burton as a butcher's boy and, following First World War service, he worked for GB Matthews at the brewery until his retirement in 1956. He was a very public-spirited citizen and was also involved with the British Legion, Silver Band and the football club.

Below: 'Spivs' Robert Budd and Terry Lush operate in Station Road on Carnival Day, *c.* 1955.

Ted Willis celebrates his ninetieth birthday at the Haig Club (now the Royal British Legion), *c.* 1960. From left to right, back row: Mick O'Dea, Bill Slade, Sid Carter, Archie Rose. Front row: Mr Gould, Ted Jones, Kim Comben, Ted Willis.

The Buffalo darts team, 1940s. The team includes: Joe Dolman, Archie Doggrell, Mark Fry, Reg Cross, Cyril Sims and ? White.

The Fir Tree pub's outing to Weston-Super-Mare, 1946. The Fir Tree was situated on the Mere Road and is now a private residence.

Coronation Club presentation night supper, 1950s.

Gillingham Jazz Band, 1927. The band raised funds to restart the old Town Band, which has been going strong ever since.

Phil Wiseman & The Travellers, 1958. From left to right: Dave Bennett, Tony Martin, Sam Pike, Phil Wiseman, Ken Newport, Dave Wathen and Mervyn Miles.

Swimming bath in Hardings Lane, 1960. This was opened in June 1959 and dedicated to 'Those Who Served 1939-1945'. Funds raised by the Welcome Home Committee were invested and eventually used for this worthwhile project. The baths are now covered and part of the Leisure Centre.

Hockey team, 1955. From left to right, back row: Theresa Suter, Joyce Foster, Marion Blanchard, Sally Pike, Hazel Flower, Vera Collis. Front row: Molly Griffiths, Yvonne Birchall, Janet Smart, Beryl Knapton, Helen Burt. Bill Foster is the umpire.

Preparations in Station Road for the visit of the as-yet-uncrowned Queen Elizabeth and Prince Philip, 1952. After leaving the station, the princess would proceed to Mere via Station Road, High Street, Queen Street, Bay Road and Lawn Cross Road. Over the next ten years, she made several unofficial visits to the National Stud at Sandley. The next official visit was not until 1990, on her way to see her grandchildren at Port Regis School.

Visit of Her Majesty the Queen on 3 July 1952. The Queen arrived at Gillingham station at 2.15pm. The Earl of Shaftesbury, Lord Lieutenant of the County, presented Mr E. Batho (chairman of the parish council) and Mr F.W. Davis (clerk to the parish council). Large numbers of local school children greeted the Queen outside the station entrance. Elizabeth King, who was accompanied by Isobel Case, presented a bouquet of flowers from the schools. In the background is Mrs Brocklebank, who presented a specially bound copy of *The Mam'll Book*.

Local dignitaries raise a glass to toast Sherman's new building in Station Road. Mr George Hoy, founder and chairman, laid a commemorative stone on 7 May 1975.

Shermans' Christmas Dinner, c. 1964. From left to right, back row (standing): Trevor Howard, Ken Tottle, Geoff Hacker, Bob Biss, Tom ?, Richard Gould. Back row (seated): Mr and Mrs Webster, Herbert Hoy, Mrs Hoy, George and Mrs Hoy, Mr and Mrs Howard. Other diners: -?-, George Davis, Robert Simpson, John Ayres, Mrs Case Mr Case, Barry Whittaker, Ron Kemp, Tony Ritchen, Pam Collis, Mr and Mrs Wiles, Ray Gulliford. Ann Tregurtha, Chris Marsh, Mrs Marsh, Kath Anker, Pete Towndrow, -?-, Pam Dyke, Pat Pickford, Sid Pickford, Bert King.

Gillingham Brownies at the 1964 carnival, commemorating fifty years of their organisation. From left to right: Julia Johnson, Carol Dear, Sue Moore, Evelyn Stokes, Margret Welbourne, Alison Hardy, Rachel Suttle, Sandra Weeks, Jane Gurnett, Anita Scott, -?-, Rachel Green, Clare Luffman, Anne Newcombe, Penny Abbot and Angela Rice.

The Youth Club football team, 1974. Back row, from left to right: Colin Lucas, Robert Gray, Mark Farrand, Mike Loader, Ray Miles, Bob Biss, Robert Smith, Tommy Biss. Front row: Gerald Matthews, Dave Hardiman, Mike Lloyd, Dave Hoskins, Owen Pritchard, Stuart Hacker, John Hillier.

Rover Scouts and Senior Scouts belonging to St Mary's Troop with the group scoutmaster,
Canon E.L. Seager, about to set off for a fortnight's holiday in Brittany, August 1955.

Floods in the High Street, July 1982.

Herbie, Alan and John Light of W.H. Light & Co., Newbury, 1950s. Formerly makers of the Magnet cycle and suppliers of motorcycles, it is today a Texaco garage.

The mill, showing flood and fire damage, 1982.

Wiles Bakery, Hardings Lane, 1948.

Clearing up the river and river bank, 1970s. The War Memorial was later removed to the car park and the buildings in the background were demolished in 1996.

Gillingham Town Council, 1977. From left to right, back row: -?-, E. Samways, M. Osmond, F. Shepherd (clerk), F. Evill, Mrs K. DeGruchy, T. Raisebeck, Mrs C. Raisebeck, R. Weeks, C. Howe, Mrs H. Burt. Front row: S. Hiscott, A. Coombs, S. Ballard (mayor), G. Jones.

Committee and helpers of the Local History Society on the day the new museum was officially opened by society president, Herbert Green, October 1996. From left to right: David Lloyd (vice-chairman), John Juddery, Alan Whiffen, Joan Jaggard, Mr Coates, Peter Crocker (chairman), Glyn Crocker, Nigel Gates (asst. curator), Mrs Dowle (librarian), Lyn Light (curator), Herbie Light, Ken Fisher, Library Asst, John Pinnock, Ralph Allman (secretary), Pearl Coates, Bob Walton and Dave Hiscock. Gillingham Museum became the first recipient of a Heritage Lottery Award.

PENGUIN
SPECIALS

Penguin Specials fill a gap. Written by some of today's most exciting and insightful writers, they are short enough to be read in a single sitting – when you're stuck on a train; in your lunch hour; between dinner and bedtime. Specials can provide a thought-provoking opinion, a primer to bring you up to date, or a striking piece of fiction. They are concise, original and affordable.

To browse digital and print Penguin Specials titles, please refer to **www.penguin.com.au/penguinspecials**

Beethoven in China

How the great composer
became an icon in the
People's Republic

JINDONG CAI AND
SHEILA MELVIN

PENGUIN BOOKS

UK | USA | Canada | Ireland | Australia
India | New Zealand | South Africa | China

Penguin Books is part of the Penguin Random House group of companies
whose addresses can be found at global.penguinrandomhouse.com.

This edition first published by Penguin Group (Australia)
2015

1 3 5 7 9 10 8 6 4 2

Cover design by Di Suo © Penguin Group (Australia)
Text design by Steffan Leyshon-Jones © Penguin Group (Australia)
Printed and bound in China in Hong Kong by Printing Express

penguin.com.au

ISBN: 9780734399526

CONTENTS

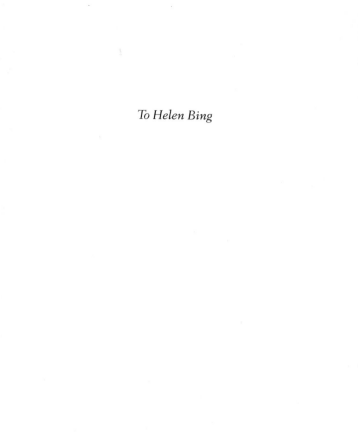

To Helen Bing

Jindong's Preface

One autumn afternoon in the dull middle years of the Cultural Revolution (1966–76), my friend and classmate Wang Luyan approached me with a whispered invitation to go home with him after school and play old records on a wind-up phonograph.

I knew this wasn't allowed; during the Cultural Revolution we were taught to 'destroy the old and build the new', and were only supposed to listen to model operas or revolutionary songs. But Luyan and I regularly read banned books, like Dumas' *La Dame aux Camélias* and Tolstoy's *Anna Karenina*, always with the covers torn off and a three-day time limit because someone else was waiting for it. If we didn't have a good novel we would spend hours fiddling with our outlawed shortwave radios, tweaking the dial infinitesimally and straining to hear the songs that signalled the start of a broadcast by Radio Moscow ('Song of the Motherland') or Voice of America ('Yankee Doodle'). So it was without hesitation that I walked with Luyan to his family's courtyard house at Dongmencang, in the shadow of Beijing's 600-year-old Imperial Granary.

The phonograph was kept in the northern chamber, the sunny, south-facing room in a courtyard house. We entered the room and shuttered the windows, just as we would do when listening to the shortwave. Luyan inserted the big needle into the arm, wound the crank and put on a Victor 78 RPM recording of the most rebellious thing kids like us could listen to in an era when 'bourgeois' music of the 'exploiting' classes was strictly forbidden: Beethoven.

I still remember the sound of the ancient needle scratching the grooves of the battered record – *swoosh, swoosh, swoosh*. But I was transfixed by the music itself, which was so big and so powerful. Hearing Beethoven for the first time that afternoon was a transformational moment: it helped set me on the path to become a musician.

In July 1976, a horrific earthquake hit northern China, killing at least 250 000 people at the epicentre in Tangshan. Hundreds in my hometown of Beijing also died and in the aftermath we had to live in make-shift tents for months while waiting for buildings to be declared safe. There wasn't much to do, so I went to libraries to see if I could find any music books – and discovered one day, to my surprise, that the stacks in the Dongcheng District Library had quietly reopened after being closed during the Cultural Revolution.

I wandered through the music section and found a yellowing, paperbound translation of Robert Haven Schauffler's *Beethoven: The Man Who Freed Music* that had been published in the 1930s. Its cover had a reproduction of Joseph Karl Stieler's famous portrait of Beethoven, fierce-browed, standing before a grove of trees and gripping a pen as he composes the 'Missa Solemnis'. The epigraph, a quote from Beethoven, is one I have always remembered: 'He who truly understands my music must thereby go free of all the misery which others bear about with them.'

I took the book back to our tent and read it in the murky light of the streetlamps on Workers' Stadium Road, suddenly hopeful that things might be changing, and that in my life I might have the opportunity to understand Beethoven's music and maybe even to perform his symphonies some day.

The Cultural Revolution ended a few months after the earthquake and in 1979 I had the opportunity to hear Beethoven performed in Beijing by some of the world's top orchestras, including the Berlin Philharmonic under Herbert von Karajan, and the Boston Symphony under

Seiji Ozawa. Karajan hardly moved when he conducted Beethoven's Seventh – his eyes were closed. His energy *was* completely contained within him, yet he had absolute control of the orchestra. The sound produced was brilliant and astounding – I had never heard a live orchestra make music like that. When Ozawa conducted the Fifth, there was rhythm in every part of his body and music in his every movement, as if his body *was* the music.

Ozawa conducted the China Central Philharmonic's performance of the Ninth later that year – I was so overwhelmed by the music that I jumped on stage and got him to autograph my program before the security guards could catch me. I still have the program, to which I also added my own youthful response to the performance: 'It seems like my entire heart, my entire being, has dissolved into this magnificent, glorious symphony . . . Beethoven is unmatchable . . . This is real music – its power makes me forget everything.'

Watching these great maestros perform Beethoven inspired me to become a conductor.

The impact Beethoven had on me was not unique. Since his music was first introduced to China in the early twentieth century, generations of Chinese have been inspired by Beethoven's story of triumph over adversity, and stirred by his works. Artists and intellectuals, reformers and revolutionaries, Confucians and Communists, student protesters and government cadres have all adopted Beethoven to promote their often contradictory goals.

Of course, this is true the world over – Beethoven's music has been appropriated by saints and sinners alike, its perceived universality making it fair game for almost any cause. But there is no parallel to the depth and breadth of Beethoven's integration into the culture, politics and private passions of China, a nation of people whose geography, history, philosophy and musical traditions are so distant from those of the Europe that produced and sustained the great composer.

Initially, Beethoven was presented to the Chinese public as a sage-like figure – a sort of modern, musical Confucius. Later, he was portrayed as a revolutionary. Mao Zedong attended at least one performance of Beethoven's music, and his wife – for whom I once conducted a youth orchestra in the Great Hall of the People – developed an odd fixation on the composer's Sixth Symphony. Premier Zhou Enlai made a private study of all nine Beethoven symphonies because he wanted to choose one that Henry Kissinger would like to hear. Former president Jiang Zemin has said that it is not good if the Chinese people know nothing about Beethoven's Ninth Symphony; in truth, many know much more. Romain Rolland's *Life of Beethoven* has been required reading in Chinese middle schools for years; his ten-volume novel *Jean-Christophe*, which is based on the life of Beethoven, was one of the most popular foreign novels in twentieth-century China. I read it in the early 1980s, as did almost all my friends.

Nowadays, books like *Beethoven, My Great Model* are are often given to children to encourage them to work hard and surmount their challenges. One wealthy Chinese entrepreneur has even titled her memoir *Beethoven's Descendant* because she credits the composer with inspiring her success. Public statues of foreigners in China are rare – with the exception of Beethoven, whose wild-haired countenance cast in bronze can be found in cities across the nation. Orchestras throughout China play Beethoven countless times each year – his work is almost certainly performed more frequently than that of any other Western composer. China even has an amateur orchestra and chorus (whom I have rehearsed) comprised exclusively of top-ranking Communist cadres, military officials and intelligentsia who travel around the country performing for Chinese citizens in concerts that conclude with Beethoven's 'Ode to Joy', sung in its original German.

While an interest in Beethoven is now benign, even expected, this has not always been the case. During the Cultural Revolution, kids like me could do pretty much what we wanted – so long as we didn't get caught – but the intellectuals and artists who did the most to bring

Beethoven to China suffered terribly for their efforts. Some even paid with their lives. Beethoven helped make me who I am, and he helped make China what it is today.

This book is the story of how and why Beethoven became a personal, political and musical icon in the People's Republic – China's sage of music.

Jindong Cai
June 2015

I

A New Sage for China

Ludwig van Beethoven (1770–1827) was introduced to China by a series of remarkable artists and intellectuals who separately 'discovered' the German composer during overseas sojourns. These men lived in the early twentieth century, a tumultuous era in which the foundations of traditional Chinese society were crumbling. They were drawn to Beethoven for a variety of reasons, among them his compelling personal story of struggle, suffering and triumph; his moral philosophy, expressed in statements such as 'I recognise no sign of superiority in mankind other than goodness'; the esteem in which he was held in Europe, the United States and Japan; and the powerful mystique of his music. But they shared one overarching goal, which they hoped Beethoven might help them achieve: to change China.

'The Romantic Patriot', Li Shutong

The first person to write about Beethoven for a Chinese audience was a brilliant polymath and versatile artist named Li Shutong (1880–1942). Li was born in the coastal city of Tianjin to a wealthy family of salt merchants and bankers. His father, known as 'Li the Good' because of his charitable undertakings, had four wives; Li's mother, who was nearly fifty years her husband's junior, was the fourth.

The young Li was given a traditional education in the Confucian classics but he became interested in politics around 1898, when the Guangxu Emperor implemented a series of radical political and cultural reforms after China was defeated in an 1895 war with Japan. The far-reaching reform effort failed after just 104 days, when the Emperor's conservative aunt, the Empress Dowager Cixi, put him under house arrest. (It is widely believed that she later had him poisoned.)

Disappointed, Li moved to Shanghai to further his education and find his own way to help reform China. He enrolled in the progressive Nanyang Public School, where he studied economics and was tutored in Japanese by the renowned educator Cai Yuanpei. In his free time he wrote and published poetry, performed in amateur Peking opera productions and worked as a journalist. He also indulged himself, as a friend later put it, 'in the world of wine and poetry. He was like a white butterfly that had been let loose in the vast flower patch that was Shanghai, and he constantly flitted in and out of damasked chambers . . .'[1] In 1905 Li went to Japan, as did thousands of young intellectuals who hoped to see for themselves how and why China's disdained Asian neighbour had grown strong while China itself had become weak.

Over the course of the nineteenth century, China had lost several wars to Britain and France, fought in part over the British insistence that its merchants be permitted to sell opium to the Chinese people. The 'unequal treaties' that followed these defeats forced China to open its doors to foreign trade, investment, settlement, religious proselytising and the devastating drug trade. In 1860 a combined force of British and French soldiers looted the Qing Dynasty's Yuanmingyuan residence, a vast series of hundreds of palaces nestled among sprawling grounds that harboured theatres, temples, libraries, pavilions, gazebos and galleries filled with priceless art, antiquities, books, religious objects and personal belongings. When the pillage was complete, the British forces burnt it to the ground.

The Qing Dynasty's sovereignty steadily eroded as foreign nations began to carve China up 'like a ripe melon', establishing 'concessions' in which foreign laws prevailed and Chinese were second-class citizens. In 1900 an anti-foreign martial arts society began to attack foreign legations, missionaries and Chinese Christians; the beleaguered Empress Dowager cast her lot with the rebels, hoping they would oust the foreigners. Instead, eight foreign powers formed an army that crushed the uprising, occupied Beijing and demanded huge reparations.

In desperation, the Qing government dusted off the reforms it had abandoned, and in 1905 took the radical step of abolishing the imperial examination system that had been used for centuries to select civil servants.[2] The exam was based on Confucian classics, ancient poetry and archaic essay structures; it completely ignored engineering and science. The system aimed to select upright men who were 'obedient to their elders', who prized uniformity of thinking and rigid adherence to Confucian orthodoxy, and who disdained creativity and individual thinking, all of which were increasingly seen as being out of step with the needs of the nation.

The decision to abolish the exam was forward-looking, but it meant that the millions of young men who had spent years memorising obscure Confucian texts and writing contrived 'eight-legged essays' in the hope of passing the test and becoming a civil servant found their entire education rendered meaningless. In a remarkably bold move, the government encouraged these young people to go abroad and learn from the very nations that were assailing China. By 1906 some 13000 young Chinese, including Li Shutong, were in Japan to pursue a new kind of education and forge a new path for themselves and for their nation.

Li enrolled in the Tokyo University of the Arts, where he studied under the famous French-educated impressionist Kuroda Seiki, the 'father of oil painting in Japan'.[3] In a life drawing class, Li was discomfited when he encountered nude models for the first time. However, he appears to have adapted quickly: before long he had asked his landlord's daughter to pose naked for him.[4] A self-portrait Li painted during this time shows a handsome, moustachioed man with thick hair and eyebrows, high cheekbones, full lips and a dreamy expression standing before a forest painted with dabs of colour. Another painting from around the same time – which caused a national sensation when it was discovered in a Beijing storehouse in 2011 – depicts a half-naked woman resting serenely in a chair, her eyes shut and a fan in her hand. Perhaps this was the landlord's daughter, who became Li's lover not long after she posed for him.[5]

When he wasn't painting, Li wrote about art, practised calligraphy and founded the first Chinese theatrical group dedicated to the performance of Western-style spoken drama. (Chinese drama, such as Peking opera, was traditionally sung.) Li played Marguerite in a performance of *La Dame aux Camélias* directed by the famous Japanese actor Asajiro Fujisawa, and acted another female role in a stage adaptation of Harriet Beecher Stowe's *Uncle Tom's Cabin*. These were political acts: Lin Shu, the writer who introduced both stories to the Chinese public through elegant retellings, compared the status of Chinese labourers in America to that of black slaves, and stated explicitly that he intended *Uncle Tom's Cabin* as a warning against the danger of white racism, which he feared would enslave Asians as it had Africans unless the Chinese people woke up and resisted it.

Li also became interested in Western music, which played a critical aspect in the cultural reform program that followed Japan's forced opening to the West. The Meiji Emperor, who by 1876 had his own symphony orchestra, sent a delegation to the United States that came back eager to promote music education in Japanese schools. Working together in the early 1880s, the Japanese reformer Isawa Shuji and the renowned American music educator Luther Whiting Mason created a series of music textbooks that included dozens of nineteenth-century European and American hymns, folk songs and classical melodies set to Japanese texts. These didactic 'school songs' became a key part of elementary education and made a big impression on

Li, who saw that they could be used for pedagogical and patriotic purposes in Chinese schools, which at the time included no formal music instruction.

We don't know how Li first encountered Beethoven but it could have been through his study of these school songs, since some were set to melodies borrowed from Beethoven. Li would also have read about Beethoven in the many Japanese journals that promoted and explained Western classical music; a magazine called *Music* published the entire score to Beethoven's 'Moonlight' Sonata the year Li arrived in Tokyo.[6] It's also possible, although less likely, that Li heard the composer's music performed in a concert setting; Beethoven's work premiered in Japan in 1887, when a Dutch conductor led a student ensemble in the andante of the First Symphony,[7] but performances remained rare. The Third Symphony was first performed in Tokyo in 1908, for example, and the Fifth in 1920.

In any case, in 1906 Li wrote an article introducing Beethoven to the Chinese public; he also drew a likeness of the composer, a charcoal sketch showing Beethoven with a firm jaw, resolute brow and wild hair. Both were published in the premiere (and only) issue of *The Little Music Magazine*, the first Chinese magazine about music, which Li founded, edited and published in Tokyo, but circulated in Shanghai. Li hinted at his political goals on the cover, which included a watercolour of opium poppies and several bars of 'La Marseillaise', the revolutionary French anthem to freedom – a suggestion, perhaps, that he hoped to pry his fellow Chinese away from the lassitude of opium and urge them towards political activism.[8]

Left: Charcoal drawing of Beethoven by Li Shutong
Right: Li Shutong

The title he gave to his article about Beethoven was equally revealing: 'The Sage of Music'. Li was a reformer but also a product of Confucian society, and he believed in the importance of moral exemplars and knew that China needed new ones. Music had been equated with morality in China since time immemorial – Confucius had advised that man could be 'perfected by music'. However, while music was seen as a force of moral good (or bad) and employed as a tool of governance, musicians themselves held little status – all the veneration went to men of letters. Composers were craftsmen rather than artists, and their names were rarely even recorded; professional musicians held roughly the same social position as servants.

Li and other early music reformers admired the respectful Western approach to composers, which tended to emphasise creativity and individuality, and the struggle and suffering required to achieve greatness – all qualities which China would need if it was to stand up in the world. They hoped to import music that would inspire their fellow citizens to greatness: they would borrow what they saw as Japan's successful adaptation of Western music, raise the status and quality of musicians in China and provide a new sort of moral exemplar – or sage – for a changing world. Beethoven fit the bill perfectly.[9]

Li's essay on Beethoven emphasised the composer's life story, introducing him simply as 'a German born in Bonn'. He explained that Beethoven's 'talent was shown when he was young', and that he worked as a musician from the age of thirteen, but he omitted the composer's stormy (and un-Confucian) relationship with his alcoholic father. 'Beethoven was profound, reticent and melancholic,' Li wrote. 'He disliked meeting other people. He was totally different from Mozart, who was humorous and amusing. He was honest, sincere and profound.'[10]

Li noted that Beethoven repeatedly edited and revised his compositions and criticised his own mistakes. His life was hard: 'He remained single for life. He suddenly went deaf in the prime of his life. In 1800, his deafness grew so serious that he could not hear any music.' Li emphasised Beethoven's loneliness by explaining that, in old age, he had lived with his niece. (In fact, Beethoven had intermittent custody of his nephew, Karl.) 'He became even more depressed due to his niece's indecency. Tiredness easily causes illness, depression does harm.' Li touched on Beethoven's music only at the end of the essay, explaining that it was divided into three periods and was much like that of his predecessors, differentiated primarily by 'the genuine feelings and wholeheartedness shown in his works, and the perfect organization of structure'.

Li returned to China (accompanied by his landlord's daughter) in 1911, just in time to see the Qing Dynasty overthrown. The imperial system that had united China for millenia collapsed, and the Republic of China was established with Sun Yat-sen (1866–1925) as its first provisional president.

Li stayed the course and became a reforming educator. He taught art students to sketch from actual objects, rather than to copy and trace, and caused a firestorm when he introduced nude models to the classroom. He helped bring staff notation, piano accompaniment and choral training to Chinese schools.[11] He wrote words or music for about 100 school songs, usually penning the lyrics himself and setting them to popular American tunes or themes from operas, symphonies, sonatas or concertos by European composers. He set at least three songs to themes from Beethoven, including the Piano Sonata in E Minor (Op. 90), the Violin Concerto in D Major (Op. 61) and the Ninth Symphony.

The political and economic situation in China continued to deteriorate as the new government failed to consolidate power, regional warlords grew strong and the country became increasingly fragmented. Li eventually abandoned hope of reforming his country through art and music. In 1916 he went to the Running Tiger of Great Kindness Buddhist Temple and fasted for seventeen days. Two years later he returned to the temple, where he shaved his head, renounced all his worldly ties and become a monk known as Dharma Master Hongyi.

In this incarnation, Li became an expert at interpreting Buddhist texts and deciphering monastic codes. He lectured at temples across southern China and practised calligraphy. The last inscription he wrote before his death in 1942 was one that Beethoven would surely have appreciated: 'Worldly joys and sorrows are intertwined.'

The May Fourth Generation

Li Shutong's essay on Beethoven was influential primarily among a small circle of like-minded intellectuals, especially those who had also studied in Japan. It lit a torch which was picked up and carried forward by other reformers, who can loosely be grouped together as members of the May Fourth generation.

The date 4 May 1919 refers to a student demonstration staged in Beijing to protest the Chinese government's response to the Treaty of Versailles, which ended the First World War. Between 1916 and 1922 China sent 135000 men to France and Belgium to support the Allied war effort by laying railway lines, repairing tanks, collecting corpses and digging the graves of fallen European soldiers.[12] In return for this assistance, China expected the Allied powers to ensure that Germany's concessions in Shandong Province – which had been taken over by Japan during the war – would be returned to China. When this did not happen, many Chinese felt betrayed by the West and what they saw as its lip-service to freedom and democracy – and let down by their own government. Protests broke out, workers began to strike and the official Chinese representative at Versailles, V. K. Wellington Koo, ultimately refused to sign the treaty.

More broadly, the term May Fourth refers to an era of cultural upheaval and experimentation, of political activism and intellectual foment; Mao Zedong later called it 'a new stage in China's bourgeois-democratic revolution against imperialism and feudalism', which 'went a step beyond the Revolution of 1911'.[13] During this period, an increasing number of intellectuals began to question the value of their nation's millennia-old culture, and even to suggest that it had made China weak. They wanted to throw off the shackles of Chinese tradition and import the culture that had made the West so strong.

In 1919 these sentiments were articulated by Lu Xun, a writer now known as the father of modern Chinese literature: 'It is better to admire Darwin and Ibsen rather than Confucius and Guan Yu; it is better to be sacrificed to Apollo rather than to the General of the Plague and the God of Five Spheres.'[14] Lu Xun also promoted Beethoven, albeit briefly, in a widely read essay on the history of science, penned while he was studying in Japan. He described science as 'the holy light that illuminates the world',[15] but emphasised that culture was just as important – with all his examples taken from the West. 'What humanity should hope for and demand,' he wrote, 'is not only Newton but also poets like Shakespeare; not only Boyle, but also Raphaelo, not only Kant, but also Beethoven, not only Darwin, but also Carlyle.'[16]

The poet Xu Zhimo crystallised this attitude in a 1922 speech entitled 'Art and Life':

> We have no art precisely because we have no life. With all our virtues and qualities, we Chinese as a race have never realized and expressed ourselves completely, as the Greeks and Romans did, through the medium of art – which is the consciousness of life . . .
>
> Isn't it significant that none of our poets, with the only possible exception of Li Po, can be said to be of cosmic character? Isn't it striking that we look in vain in the scroll of our literary fames for even the least resemblance of a Goethe, a Shelley, a Wordsworth even not to say Dante and Shakespeare? And as for the other arts, who is there here to rank with the vast genius of men like Michelangelo, Leonardo da Vinci, Turner, Corregio, Velasquez, Wagner, Beethoven – to name but a few? . . .
>
> We possess an artistic heritage, essentially inferior to that of the West, in that it fails to comprehend life as a whole.[17]

Other May Fourth intellectuals delved deeper into the study of Western music in general and Beethoven in particular, certain that both might help bring change to China. Feng Zikai, a multi-talented artist and disciple of

Li Shutong, wrote or translated a number of books about music, including *The Life and Art of Two Contemporary Composers* (1930), *Ten Great Musicians of Modern Times* (1929) and *Great Composers and Masterpieces of the World* (1931).[18] All these books included Beethoven, but the first, on Beethoven and Schubert, contained the most comprehensive discussion of the composer to date.

Feng, like Li, emphasised Beethoven's life story and moral qualities. He described the adversities Beethoven had faced, and suggested that it was his character that had helped him overcome them. Beethoven, in Feng's characterisation, was not only a great musician but also a 'hero' to all mankind. He compared Beethoven to Napoleon – they were the two great heroes of late eighteenth-century Europe – but claimed that while Napoleon would be forgotten, Beethoven would be remembered forever because life is short, but art eternal.[19] Feng even recalled the composer Richard Wagner's belief that Beethoven had the same importance to music that Shakespeare had to literature, and Jesus to religion. (Wagner also supposedly said, 'A greater than I exists. It is Beethoven.'[20]) Having established Beethoven's place in history (perhaps with some exaggeration), Feng devoted two full chapters to explaining his music, discussing all nine symphonies and thirty-two piano sonatas.

Another scholar and writer, the Sichuan-born Wang Guangqi, began the process of 'localising' Beethoven so that Chinese could better relate to him. Wang lived in Germany from 1920 until his death in 1936, studying music at Berlin University – the composer Carl Orff was one of his teachers – and eventually moving to Bonn, Beethoven's birthplace, to study for a doctorate. He came to believe that Germany's rich musical culture had played a major role in its transformation to become a powerful modern state, and that classical music might help his own country reinvent itself and emerge as a 'young China'.[21]

In his book *Introduction to Western Musical Masterpieces*, Wang explained that Beethoven was deaf in both ears, struggled with illness and was plagued by frustration, grief and indignation, but that he nonetheless managed to compose the eternal masterpiece that is the Ninth Symphony. Wang placed Beethoven in a Chinese context by comparing him to Sima Qian (c. 145–86 BCE), the esteemed historian who was castrated for his defence of a general wrongly accused of treason. Castration was then considered a fate worse than death, and Sima chose it out of filial piety, so he could complete his father's monumental work *Records of the Grand Historian*. Wang was drawing an analogy between Beethoven's deafness and Sima's painful and humiliating emasculation – and simultaneously according Beethoven the elevated status enjoyed by one of China's greatest heroes.[22]

II

The Sound of Beethoven

Even as idealistic reformers who believed passionately in the transformative power of classical music were promoting Beethoven through their writing, the composer's music was being performed in China for the first time. But in a sad irony, these performances took place in an exclusive expatriate domain that was closed to Chinese. Only when the separate worlds of foreigners and Chinese merged could the two versions of Beethoven – one a musical sage to be read about in books, and the other a composer whose music could inspire – become one.

Foreign Foundations

Christian missionaries laid the foundation required for the performance of Beethoven in China: the Catholics by promoting an image of Western music as advanced, scientific and elite, and the Protestants (who came later) by popularising choral singing, the harmonium and the piano – and some rudimentary Beethoven – in the schools and churches they established.

This process started as early as 1307, when the Franciscan friar John of Montecorvino travelled to Beijing, got himself declared its archbishop and, in his words, 'gradually bought one hundred and fifty boys, the children of pagan parents, and of ages varying from seven to eleven'.[23] He taught these children Greek and Latin, and formed a choir. According to the friar, 'His Majesty the Emperor moreover delights much to hear them chanting.'

In 1601 the Jesuit Matteo Ricci gave a clavichord to the Ming Dynasty's Wanli Emperor. Ricci knew that China did not have keyboard instruments and figured the Emperor would be intrigued – which he was. This began a missionary tradition of presenting Western musical instruments to the throne and teaching Western music at court; on several occasions Chinese emperors even wrote directly to Catholic popes to request more music instructors. A Jesuit account notes that the Qing Dynasty's Kangxi Emperor was dumbfounded when he saw the Portuguese Jesuit Thomas Pereira jot down with staff notation Chinese tunes he had heard only once, and then play them back on a harpsichord. '"It must be owned," cry'd the Emperor, "the European Music is incomparable, and this father has not his equal in all the Empire.'"[24]

Protestant missionaries began arriving after the Opium Wars, and their numbers accelerated at the turn of the twentieth century. They formed churches with choruses and schools in which they taught music. By 1908 Chinese choruses from missionary schools were singing hymns like 'Sing with All the Sons of Glory', with music from Beethoven's 'Ode to Joy'.[25]

In 1925 a missionary from Ohio named Bliss Wiant performed Beethoven in a most unusual venue: at the funeral of Sun Yat-sen, the Republic of China's founding father. Wiant was asked to take charge of the music for Sun's private Christian funeral, which was held in the chapel of Peking Union Medical College at 10 a.m. on 19 March 1925. Wiant trained a group of religious students to sing Dr Sun's favourite hymn, and as a prelude performed the second movement of Beethoven's Third Symphony, a majestic, tragic funeral march. 'As I played the organ,' he later wrote, 'the faces of many folk anxious to witness this event, were pressed against the windowpane opposite the organ bench.'[26] Wiant went on to spend nearly thirty years teaching music in China, and over that period taught Chinese students to perform many great Western choral works, including Beethoven's Ninth and several of the composer's shorter vocal works.

But if missionaries had laid the foundation for an

interest in classical music, it was the Westerners who travelled to or settled in China for secular reasons who did the most to promote it – initially, simply because they themselves wanted to hear it. The Shanghai Public Band was founded in 1879 by the city's foreign residents; eventually it became the Shanghai Municipal Orchestra, and then the Shanghai Symphony Orchestra. In its early years it was comprised entirely of Filipino musicians – then known as 'Manila men' – and was primarily a wind ensemble with a small string orchestra. Complaints about the band's performance were constant, but it was nonetheless considered an essential element of civic life. In 1906 a committee of 'gentlemen' interested in music prepared a report for the municipal council that affirmed the band's importance to Shanghai's cultural life:

> Amongst the many intellectual and refined pleasures open to the public in the home countries, such as high class dramatic art, opera, art galleries, collections, and good orchestral music, only the last named is at present within the reach of our Settlement. It therefore seems in the true interest of the Shanghai Community that a special effort should be made to produce something really good in this respect which may atone for the lack of nearly all the other enjoyments of the same kind.[27]

However, the committee also noted: 'It is the unanimous opinion that the performances of the Town Band during the last years have been far from satisfactory. As a rule, the music selected has been rather trivial, the rendering indifferent, and the intonation often painfully at fault.'[28] The committee blamed a bad conductor, poor instruments and the Filipino musicians, who, 'not being in possession of the same physical strength as Europeans', could not 'sustain their notes with the same degree of efficiency'.[29] It suggested the solution would be to create an entire orchestra of musicians from Europe; that would be too expensive, so the next best thing was to recruit a European conductor and musicians to lead the instrument sections. Later that year, a conductor named Rudolf Buck arrived from Berlin with six German musicians and began the process of transforming the band into an orchestra that played Beethoven.

The earliest surviving program dates to the 1911–12 winter season, and includes the finale from Beethoven's Third Symphony ('Eroica', or 'Heroic Symphony'), which the composer initially thought to dedicate to Napoleon. All told, Buck conducted Beethoven eight times that season.[30] However, because of the racism of the era and the quasi-colonial nature of Shanghai's International Settlement and French Concession, Chinese were not allowed into the venues where the orchestra performed. This state of affairs continued until Buck departed

Shanghai in 1918. He was replaced in 1919 by a charismatic Italian named Mario Paci, who threatened to quit unless the council allowed Chinese to attend concerts, which it finally did in 1925. Soon about a quarter of the concert audience was Chinese.[31]

Paci had trained as a pianist since childhood but as a young man decided to become a conductor. He went to Milan to enrol in the city's famed conservatory, but was too scared to take the exam. While hanging around Milan studying music theory, he was asked to play for guests at a party attended by musical luminaries including the composer Giacomo Puccini. Paci's interpretation of Beethoven's 'Appassionata' Sonata – described by Beethoven's early biographer Wilhelm von Lenz as 'a volcanic eruption, which rends the earth and shuts out the sky with a shower of projectiles' – so impressed Puccini that he offered to write him a recommendation. It read: 'Young Paci presents himself at the examination but is not prepared. Do not waste time with questions on the "prohibited Fifths". Have him play Beethoven's 'Appassionata' and I am sure you will not want to lose a fine future pupil.'[32] It worked: the conservatory's examiners smiled when they read Puccini's note, asked Paci to play Beethoven and admitted him to the conducting class.

Paci forever after remained loyal to Beethoven. The first recital he gave upon arriving in Shanghai in 1919 included his 'Waldstein' Sonata, and he programmed Beethoven regularly at the orchestra and taught his Chinese piano students to play the composer's works. At the last concert he conducted before the Shanghai Municipal Orchestra was disbanded by the Japanese during the Second World War, he sat down at the piano and played the 'Appassionata'. When he died in Shanghai in 1946, his piano student Dong Kuang-kuang played Beethoven's Piano Sonata No. 26 in E-flat major (Op. 81a), known as 'Les Adieux'. But the most historically significant Beethoven performance Paci gave was a March 1927 concert to commemorate the 100th anniversary of the composer's death.

Similar events were organised the world over; in New York, for example, a celebration was held at the Town Hall and attended by consuls general from ten countries, including China. These diplomats heard, and perhaps carried home, New York Governor Al Smith's message: 'To commemorate a genius of the nature of Beethoven is to increase our stature. His message, like that of Shakespeare, is universal and timeless . . . That Beethoven was a true democrat with high ethical aspirations makes his message vital for our own time.'[33]

Paci made no such grandiose political claims at the Shanghai commemoration, which included the orchestra's premiere performance of Beethoven's Ninth, also known as the 'Choral' Symphony because its last movement includes a chorus singing verses based on the German poet Friedrich Schiller's famed 'Ode to Joy'. However, while Paci was collecting scores in his office one Monday morning before the concert, history knocked on his door in the person of a young man named Tan Shuzhen. Tan came from a Christian family in the former German concession of Qingdao, in Shandong Province, and had moved to Shanghai in search of a good violin teacher. He attended the orchestra's concerts every week and knew that a Dutch violinist was on home leave. Without beating around the bush, Tan told Paci the purpose of his visit: he wanted to take the place of the absent musician, which would make him the first Chinese to play in the orchestra. Paci asked Tan a few questions and then said simply: 'Come tomorrow.'[34]

Tan got to the rehearsal early the next day. 'I didn't know where to sit,' he recalled back in the late 1990s. 'So I waited for Paci to get up on the stage. Then he saw me and said: "Second violin, inside seat."'

Tan took the seat as directed, next to a Filipino named Mr Sato, and waited nervously until the rehearsal started. 'The music was Beethoven's Fifth – the sound was so big! *Da da da Da!* I'd never heard it so loud! It was just like a concert – we played all through without stops. Mr Sato was very good, and when it was over, Paci pointed at me and asked him, "How is he?" Mr Sato said, "He's all right." And Paci said, "Come tomorrow."'

Beethoven is said to have described the famous first phrase of his fifth symphony as 'Thus fate knocks at the door!' – an appropriate motif for the integration of China's first symphony orchestra as it played on the 100th anniversary of the composer's death.

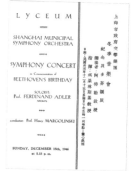

Top: The Shanghai Municipal Orchestra's Beethoven commemoration concert program, 1941

Left: A concert program commemorating Beethoven's birthday, 1946

Right: The Shanghai Symphony Orchestra's oldest program from 1911, which includes the last movement of the 'Eroica' Symphony

Great Aspirations

As the years went by, the reform-minded intellectuals of the May Fourth era journeyed further afield, and delved deeper in their effort to study the best of Western civilisation. Those who were interested in classical music no longer settled for Japan but travelled to its source – Europe, and especially Beethoven's homeland of Germany. Nor did they content themselves with writing about Beethoven and his music so Chinese could read about it; instead, they pushed for the performance of classical music in China. Perhaps the most ardent and successful promoters of reform through music – and music reform – were Xiao Youmei and Cai Yuanpei.

The son of a Confucian scholar, Xiao grew up in the Portuguese colony of Macau, in a house adjacent to that of a Portuguese priest who practised the organ at home. Xiao fell in love with the music, later writing that he regretted never learning to play the organ. In 1901 he went to Japan to pursue a degree in education at Tokyo Imperial University. While there, he also took piano and voice lessons at the Tokyo National School of Music and joined the underground resistance movement founded in 1905 by Sun Yat-sen, who was then still a revolutionary (and also a Xiao family friend). Xiao returned to China in 1909 and two years later accepted a position as Sun's presidential secretary, but in 1912 he quit and went to Leipzig, Germany.

Xiao was drawn to Leipzig because of its rich and storied musical culture. The city's Gewandhaus Orchestra is one of the oldest in the world, dating back to 1743; the composer Felix Mendelssohn led it for many years. Johann Sebastian Bach spent twenty-seven years as cantor in the city's St Thomas Church; he died and was buried in Leipzig in 1750.

Xiao enrolled at Leipzig University as a student of philosophy and education, and concurrently studied music theory and composition at the Leipzig State Conservatory of Music. He made contact with many prominent European musicians, including the Hungarian conductor Arthur Nikisch and the composer and conductor Richard Strauss.[35] After graduating in 1916 with a doctorate in music, Xiao spent another four years studying at Berlin University and the Stuttgart Conservatory of Music.[36] He became convinced that Chinese musicians should follow the examples of European composers, including Bach and Mozart, but especially the 'dignified and serious' musical sage, Beethoven.[37] In a book called *New Lives of the Music Masters*, he emphasised the hardships that European composers endured, and the extent to which their lives embodied Chinese virtues.

Cai Yuanpei – the pioneering educator who had once

taught Japanese to Li Shutong – also studied in Leipzig in 1907 and 1913. Like Xiao, with whom he became friends, Cai availed himself of every opportunity to learn, attending 'all classes in philosophy, literature, history of civilization, and anthropology, as long as they did not clash with each other, paying special attention to experimental psychology and aesthetics'.[38] His focus was the development of a theory of aesthetic education, a term he translated into Chinese as *meiyu* from the German *aesthetische Erziehung*. Cai favoured aesthetic education because he saw it as free, progressive and universal, and hoped it might one day replace religion, which he deemed coercive, conservative and restricted.[39] Cai took music-related classes at the university and regularly attended concerts; he also hired tutors to teach him the fundamentals of violin and piano.[40] He became a fan of Beethoven and wrote this little poem:

> Our nation's music is too plain,
> Westerners are surprised to hear.
> I love Beethoven's music,
> Which embodies deep and broad aspirations.[41]

Upon his return to China in 1916, Cai became president of the newly founded Peking University and began to apply the ideas he had developed in Germany. Many of these focused on the importance of research, student

36

autonomy and freedom of thought. But he also worked to implement his ideas about aesthetic education: 'since we have introduced education in the sciences,' he explained in 1919, 'we must also promote education in the arts.'[42] Because Cai saw art as transformative – capable of moulding minds and healing souls – his goal was that 'any kind of person, at all times, should have the opportunity to come into contact with art'.[43]

In 1916 Cai oversaw the creation of the Peking University Music Society (later Music Research Society) in an old Ming Dynasty building, with separate sections for Chinese and Western music. Three years later he outlined his musical goals in a speech to students, telling them he looked forward to their 'knowing that music is a good tool for the advancement of culture, working together to research into the depths of musical

Xiao Youmei with Peking University Orchestra

understanding, and cultivating talented individuals who will create new compositions, using the strengths of Western music as a supplement for the deficiencies in Chinese music'.[44]

When Xiao Youmei returned to China in 1920, Cai persuaded him to join the Music Research Society. Xiao believed in specialised, conservatory-style training of the sort he had experienced in Germany, which had the goal of 'fostering musical talent' rather than 'moulding students' temperament'.[45] He instituted a rigorous undergraduate curriculum that included music theory, composition, piano, violin and vocal music, and that also emphasised professional training.

In 1922 the Music Research Society was changed to a Music Seminar, with Cai as chair and Xiao as academic dean. Xiao worked hard to run it like a conservatory, even translating its name into English as the 'Conservatory of Music of Peking University'.[46] He created an applied music major to train professional musicians, and hired the best instrumental teachers he could find – which wasn't easy. Tan Shuzhen studied violin there in 1923 with a teacher who was primarily a clarinettist and taught Tan by singing, since Tan already played the violin better than he did. Other teachers had more experience. They included returned Chinese, such as the Swiss-trained pianist Yang Zhongzi; foreigners, such as the Russian pianist Vladimir A. Gart;[47] and former members of two famous military bands, one created by General Yuan Shikai (who replaced Sun Yat-sen as president) and the other by Robert Hart, an amateur violinist and the inspector-general of Chinese Maritime Customs.

These teachers formed the core of a small orchestra that gave twenty-nine concerts between 1922 and 1927.[48] They performed Beethoven's works more than any others: they played the Second, Third, Fifth and Sixth symphonies, the Piano Sonata No. 8 ('Pathetique') and the Egmont Overture.[49] Concerts were announced in the university newspaper and accompanied by program notes written by Xiao. When Beethoven's Third was performed, the note stated that the composer of such a heroic work had to have possessed a very high moral standard. If Beethoven were alive today, it continued, and able to see how Sun Yat-sen was upholding democracy in China, he would certainly rededicate this symphony to Sun. The program note for Beethoven's Fifth gave a similarly localised interpretation, explaining that the music depicted a struggle to emerge from a dark world into a bright one, and could thus be seen as describing China's revolutionary history over the past thirty years.[50]

Among the students drawn to the Music Research Society was a young southerner named Xian Xinghai. Xian's father died before he was born; his mother, determined to educate her son, laboured as a maid in Macao and Singapore. Thanks to her hard work, Xian was able to attend Guangdong's Lingnan University, where he studied clarinet and violin with an American teacher and learned about Beethoven from a philosophy professor. Upon graduating, Xian went to Beijing to continue his studies at the Music Research Society. He told Xiao Youmei: 'Beethoven's mother worked for rich people in the kitchen – my mother did the same. My goal is to contribute to music just like Beethoven did.'[51]

Unfortunately, ever-tightening political controls in Beijing eventually made it impossible for Cai Yuanpei to maintain the standards he had set at Peking University. In 1922 he departed for France, leaving Xiao Youmei to run the Music Seminar, until the warlord government shut it down in 1927 because musical training was a 'waste of the nation's money'.[52] Had Xiao abandoned his efforts to promote music education, the course of classical music – and the status of Beethoven – in China might have been very different. But Xiao wasn't one to give up; instead, he moved to Shanghai and founded the music school that is now the Shanghai Conservatory.

There was much Xiao disliked about Shanghai, including its commercialism and the quasi-colonial nature of the foreign presence there. He knew, however, that it was home to many foreign musicians; Shanghai, in the words of one resident, 'was swarming with musical artists by this time, all eager to play, teach, sing, act or lecture anywhere, if only an audience and pupils could be attracted'.[53] And if Shanghai could provide the teachers, Xiao knew, he could attract the pupils.

The first few classes at the conservatory were small but included some remarkable students, such as a young woman named Li Cuizhen, who arrived already able to play all thirty-two Beethoven piano sonatas from memory. Xian Xinghai also moved to Shanghai to attend the new conservatory. While there, he wrote an essay called 'Music for Everyone', in which he claimed that everyone who studied music in China 'wanted to be as influential as Beethoven, Chopin, or Wagner'. But, he said, 'it was unimaginable to have a genius who could share the limelight with Beethoven'. Xian added that Beethoven's greatness lay in his willingness to confront challenges and accept suffering; success would only come to China's music students once they, too, had cultivated this ability.[54]

III

A Friend to All Who Struggle

By the 1930s, the Beethoven of books and magazines and the Beethoven of the concert halls had become one. Chinese could now read about Beethoven, listen to his music and even perform it themselves. But so many different people had written about Beethoven that there were at least a dozen different Chinese transliterations of his name. The composer was known as *Bi Du Fen* 比獨芬; *Pei De Ke Fen* 培得訶芬; *Bei Duo Fen* 貝多忿; *Hua Tuo Fen* 華妥芬; *Fei De Fen* 斐德芬; *Bai Di Huo Fen* 白堤火分; *Pei Tuo Wen* 培陀文; *Bei Duo Wen* 悲多汶 or 貝多文; *Pei De Hua Fen* 培德花芬; *Bei Tuo Fen* 貝陀芬 and *Bei Tu Fen* 貝吐芬. This confusing smorgasbord of Beethovens was unified – as *Bei Duo Fen* 貝多芬 – only when the writer, art critic and literary translator Fu Lei turned his impassioned pen to the promotion of Beethoven in China.

The Shared Passion of Fu Lei and
Romain Rolland

Fu Lei was born in 1908 into a prosperous, land-owning family in Jiangsu's Nanhui County (now Shanghai's Pudong District). His father died at age twenty-four, when Fu was just four, and his two brothers and sister died the same year. Fu's bereaved mother was strict with her surviving son – if he misbehaved badly, she tied him to a table and made him apologise to the ancestral tablet of his dead father. In one dramatic incident, she even tried to hang herself for the shame of having raised such a disobedient son.

Although she was illiterate, Fu's mother made sure he got a first-rate classical education; she would even sit next to his teacher and memorise everything Fu was supposed to learn so she could help him review. Later, she sent him to Shanghai's Jesuit-run Saint Ignace High School. But Fu came of age in the stimulating atmosphere of the May Fourth era, and he was stubborn and strong-willed, with a rebellious spirit. He was expelled from Saint Ignace for criticising its religious practices, and came close to being arrested for participating in the anti-imperialist protests of 30 May 1925. In 1928 Fu left China to study in Paris.

For the next four years, Fu immersed himself in European cultural life, attending classes at the University of Paris and visiting art galleries around Europe. A studio photo taken in Paris shows an unsmiling Fu in round spectacles and a smart suit, waistcoat and tie. His side-parted hair hangs over his right brow and his chin rests on his hand, and he looks every bit the dapper, self-assured young intellectual. Fu was drawn to French literature and began translating short stories by writers such as Alphonse Daudet to improve his language ability. But the book that captured his imagination was a biography of Beethoven by Romain Rolland (1866–1944), winner of the 1915 Nobel Prize for Literature.

Rolland was a world-renowned writer, public intellectual and left-leaning pacifist who was then at the height of his fame. In 1931 he went to India to spend time with Mahatma Gandhi; in 1935, at the invitation of Maxim Gorky, he visited Moscow to meet Joseph Stalin. The acclaimed Austrian writer Stefan Zweig called Rolland 'the most impressive moral phenomenon of our age'. Excerpts of Rolland's work had already appeared in Chinese journals, and the poet Xu Zhimo had been similarly lavish with praise, calling Rolland 'the brave fighter for mankind', 'the spiritual and intellectual leader of the whole of Europe' and 'the fountain spring of inspiration for the entire world'.

Rolland was passionate about many things, and Beethoven was top among them. As Zweig recounted (quoting also from Rolland himself):

From Rolland's earliest years, since his beloved mother had initiated him into the magic world of music, Beethoven had been his teacher, had been at once his monitor and consoler. Though fickle to other childish loves, to this love he had ever remained faithful. 'During the crises of doubt and depression which I experienced in youth, one of Beethoven's melodies, one which still runs in my head, would reawaken in me the spark of eternal life.'[55]

As a young man, Rolland travelled to Vienna to visit the 'House of the Black Spaniard', in which Beethoven died; later, he went to Bonn to see the modest home in which Beethoven was born. He then began to research the composer's life and to write *Vie de Beethoven*. According to Zweig, Rolland's goal was 'not once again to expound the musician to musicians, but to reveal the hero to humanity at large'.

Vie de Beethoven

Rolland's biography of Beethoven opens with a quote from the composer: 'I want to prove that whoever acts rightly and nobly, can by that alone bear misfortune.' This is followed by a plea from Rolland himself: that we, the denizens of a world weighed down by 'an undignified materialism', should gather around ourselves 'the heroic friends of the past – the great souls who suffered for the good of universal humanity'. Because, Rolland continues, 'The lives of great men are not written for the proud or for the ambitious; they are dedicated rather to the unhappy. And who really is not?'

The Beethoven of Rolland's work has flashing eyes, a charming smile, dishevelled hair and a lingering aura of melancholy. In childhood his father exploits him; in adulthood his intense romantic passions fail to bear fruit, while the nephew he loves like a son turns on him. He is confident, proud and unimpressed by the rich and powerful. Rolland recounts the so-called Teplitz Incident – which became the most famous Beethoven tale in China, resonating powerfully with the May Fourth generation – in which Beethoven is strolling with his hero Goethe in the eponymous Czech spa town when the pair encounters royalty. Goethe moves to the side and bows obsequiously to let the royal party pass, while Beethoven – who genuflects only before the shrine of art – strides ahead.

While still a young man, Beethoven begins losing his noblest sense: hearing. 'But what a humiliation for me when someone standing next to me heard a flute in the distance and I heard nothing,' Beethoven wrote in his famed Heiligenstadt Testament, 'or someone standing next to me heard a shepherd singing and again I heard nothing. Such incidents drove me almost to despair; a little more of that and I would have ended my life . . .' But he does not. 'Ah, it seemed to me impossible to leave the world until I had brought forth all that I felt was within me.' Instead, he composes some of the greatest music the world has ever heard, later declaring: 'I will seize fate by the throat; it shall certainly never wholly overcome me. Oh! Life is so beautiful, would I could have a thousand lives!'[56]

Fu Lei's response to *Vie de Beethoven* mirrored Rolland's own passion for the composer. 'I burst into tears,' Fu explained, 'and suddenly felt as if I had been enlightened by the divine light and gained the power of rebirth. From that time on, I wonderfully took heart, which was indeed a great event in my whole life.'[57]

He translated the first chapter into Chinese while still in Paris, and in 1931 returned to China ready to devote himself to art, music and literature, but uncertain where to begin. He taught French and art history, founded several magazines and wrote art criticism. He married Zhu Meifu, an accomplished pianist with whom he had two sons, Fou Ts'ong (Fu Cong) and Fu Min. Fu became actively involved in his sons' education – as his mother had in his – and brought Fou Ts'ong up to be a pianist, choosing Mario Paci as his teacher. (Years later, Fou Ts'ong would make his stage debut with the Shanghai Symphony, performing Beethoven's 'Emperor' Concerto.)

Fu's return to China coincided with Japan's 1931

establishment of a puppet state in Manchuria. In January 1932 Japan bombed the working-class neighbourhood of Zhabei in Shanghai; it was one of the first terror bombings of a civilian population, preceding the Nazi attack on Guernica by five years. A battle waged for weeks, havoc reigned and thousands of innocents were killed. Fu saw a parallel between the tumultuous era in which China found itself and that of late eighteenth-century and early nineteenth-century Europe – the 'soul-stirring' era of reform and revolution in which Beethoven had emerged as a 'superstar' and an emblem of human will.

With an ink brush his only weapon, Fu secluded himself in his study and translated *Vie de Beethoven* into Chinese. In a preface, he explained that the story of Beethoven's struggle and triumph had cured his own youthful despair: when he fell down, Beethoven raised him up; when he was hurt, Beethoven comforted him; Beethoven gave him will and wisdom. He hoped that his translation of Rolland's life of Beethoven would comfort and inspire his fellow citizens in the same way it had him. 'I know of no better way,' Fu concluded, 'to repay Beethoven and his great biographer Romain Rolland for the debt I have incurred than to pass on this gift to the next generation.'[58]

Jean-Christophe

In 1937 – the year of the official outbreak of war with Japan – Fu Lei began his biggest project: a translation of Rolland's ten-volume magnum opus, *Jean-Christophe*, a cradle-to-grave bildungsroman inspired by the life of Beethoven. Fu again hoped that Beethoven – in this case, a fictionalised version – would provide courage in the midst of hardship and suffering. 'It's not a lack of darkness that makes the day bright and it's not a lack of fear that makes one a hero,' Fu wrote in his preface. 'A hero fights with fear all the time . . . When you know that other people are suffering too, you will feel less pain and your faith will be reborn from desperation.'[59] The book was 'a glorious human epic', Fu continued, and he urged readers to approach it with a 'devotional mood'.[60]

Jean-Christophe is highly romantic; as a 1915 review in put it, 'No spiritual adventure is too trivial to be remarked and no sentiment that is sincere requires apology.'[61] From the time he is born, music is Jean-Christophe's salvation – and as he grows older, he himself becomes the salvation of music:

> Everything is music for the born musician. Everything that throbs, or moves, or stirs, or palpitates – sunlit summer days, nights when the wind howls, flickering light, the twinkling of the stars, storms, the song of birds, the buzzing

of insects, the murmuring of trees, voices, loved or loathed, familiar fireside sounds, a creaking door, blood moving in the veins in the silence of the night – everything that is is music; all that is needed is that it should be heard. All the music of creation found its echo in Jean Christophe.[62]

Although Jean-Christophe is born with a God-given musical gift, he lives in a time of turmoil and is forced to surmount countless obstacles to fulfil his destiny – just like Fu's intended readers.

Fu's translation reached a million words and included hundreds of detailed footnotes that explained unfamiliar aspects of European culture, especially those related to music.[63] As he worked, Fu developed and refined the 'resemblance in spirit' theory of translation for which he became famous. 'Translation should be like copying a painting,' he wrote. 'The aim is not to produce a likeness in form but a likeness in spirit.'[64]

The first volume of Fu's translation was published in 1937, and the subsequent three volumes in 1941; ever the perfectionist, he retranslated it in 1952. The story of Jean-Christophe's quest for identity became wildly popular in progressive circles and gained what some scholars have described as a cult-like status among generations of Chinese intellectuals. These men and women in turn identified with the real-life inspiration for Jean-Christophe: Beethoven.

IV

The Challenge of Ideology

Fu Lei's loving translation of Rolland's factual and fictional paeans to Beethoven gave Chinese readers a more complete view of the composer, as a man and a musician. But even if 'Beethoven' had gradually become one person in the public eye, what he signified remained open for debate. The war with Japan and the civil war between the Communist and Nationalist parties that followed it bifurcated Beethoven anew, causing some to see the composer – and classical music generally – as representative of bourgeois decadence, while others saw him as an inspiration for revolution. This division widened after Mao Zedong gave a seminal speech on culture in 1942.

Bourgeois Beethoven

The outbreak of war had a significant impact on the young intellectuals who were Beethoven's most ardent fans. In their horror and helplessness, some responded by rejecting both the composer and the classical music of which he had become the primary representative.

At Yenching University, for instance, student protesters interrupted a choral rehearsal led by the missionary Bliss Wiant. One 'made an impassioned speech about the lack of patriotism of students who would sing when the country was in such agony'. Criticisms were lobbed at students who continued with vocal and piano practice, and protests against the school orchestra became so vehement that it suspended its activities. 'It's a very depressing time,' Wiant wrote. 'We feel that the students have taken the wrong attitude – negating everything while having nothing positive to offer. But they're closed to suggestion or advice.'[65]

A young musician named Nie Er (1912–35) perhaps best exemplifies the attitude Wiant describes, although he did in fact have something positive to offer. Nie Er grew up in the south-western province of Yunnan, where he studied English at the local YMCA. A European teacher introduced him to classical music, and Nie Er eventually decided to teach himself violin. He fell in love with the instrument and carried it everywhere he went so he could use any spare moment to practise.

On one occasion he was walking with his brother in the verdant hills that surround Kunming when they were struck by a torrential downpour. As rain coursed through the pine needles and mist shrouded the hills, the brothers huddled beneath a pagoda and Nie Er played the rousing French anthem 'La Marseillaise'. When the last note had floated away, his brother wished aloud that someone in China would compose a piece like that – and Nie Er promised him someone would.

Nie Er was also a student of Marxism, and his increasing involvement in covert Communist activities forced him to flee to Shanghai in 1930 for fear of arrest. He immersed himself in the city's musical circles, attending Shanghai Municipal Orchestra concerts, playing jazz in the Bright Moon Song and Dance Troupe and spending half his meagre monthly income on violin lessons with a renowned Czech musician named Josef Padushka.

But the bombing of Shanghai affected Nie Er deeply. He wrote down his feelings in a 7 March 1932 journal entry sprinkled with English words (in italics):

How to create revolutionary music? That's the question I've been thinking about all day, but I haven't come up with any concrete plans yet. Isn't so-called *classic* music just a plaything of the leisure class? I spend a few hours every day slaving over my basic exercises. After a few years, even a decade, I become a *violinist*. So what? Can you excite the laboring masses by playing a Beethoven *Sonata*? Will that really be an inspiration to them? No! This is a dead end. Wake up before it's too late.[66]

Nie Er did return to music, albeit with a political purpose. He composed scores of songs that reflected the lives of the downtrodden classes, often with lyrics by an influential leftist playwright named Tian Han. He also wrote music for patriotic films, including one wildly popular song called 'March of the Volunteers'; it later became China's national anthem, the country's own version of 'La Marseillaise'.

In the spring of 1935, Nie Er once again had to flee for his safety, this time to Japan. Sadly, tragedy struck not long after he arrived: the passionate young musician, at the age of just twenty-three, drowned during an outing to the beach.

Revolutionary Beethoven

Even as *Nie Er* was rejecting Beethoven, another aspiring musician named Li Delun was deciding that Beethoven and revolution were not only compatible but complementary. The gregarious and fun-loving Li came from a well-off Beijing Muslim family that ran into difficulties when an uncle turned traitor to the Japanese. Li loved music and listened to it every chance he got, parking himself by the radio for Sunday-afternoon opera broadcasts and attending every Hollywood movie half a dozen times to hear the musical accompaniments. He learned piano and violin, and in 1938 enrolled at the Catholic Furen University to study music; one foreign priest gave him an appreciation for the organ compositions of Bach, Handel and Franck, while another introduced him to *Das Kapital* and urged him to sympathise with the proletariat (which, as a member of the Communist Youth League, he already did).

In 1940 Li went to Shanghai, hoping to enrol at the conservatory. One of the first things he did on his arrival in the cosmopolitan city was go to hear the orchestra; fifty-odd years later, at the end of his life, he still remembered every musician in it, and much of what they played. Li recalled being especially excited about a program that included Beethoven's Triple Concerto; he had found the score in a used bookstore and followed it during the performance.

Li studied music in Shanghai throughout the war. To make a living, he provided live musical accompaniment for stage dramas. If there weren't enough musicians for a chamber orchestra he would play a phonograph record; soon he could tell what the music was just by looking at the grooves. After a time, he reconnected with the Communist Party, which was then 'underground' because of persecution by the Nationalists. Unfortunately, during a long night out that involved a meal, a movie, another meal and a local opera, Li lost a document that could have betrayed his political affiliation and got him arrested – or worse. His Party contacts informed him that he had to leave Shanghai for his own safety; they suggested he go to Hong Kong, but Li pleaded until they agreed to send him to the remote village of Yan'an, the Communist Party's base camp and the cradle of the revolution.

Li packed his bag – his reading material was a collection of Lu Xun's essays and the score for Beethoven's Fifth – and waited to be summoned. He was at his second job at the Voice of the USSR radio station, broadcasting Beethoven's Ninth and following along with the score, when the call came from Zhou Enlai's office in Nanjing: it was time to go to Yan'an. He left the Ninth playing, tucked the score under his arm and headed off to a new life as a revolutionary musician.

Li was flown to Yan'an on an American C-47 aircraft with a beautiful woman painted on it. The cloud cover was so thick that the pilot could not land – he asked all the passengers to move up front for ballast, and then dipped and dove until he found a place to break through to the dirt runway.

Yan'an was bleak, isolated and poor. Mao Zedong,

Zhou Enlai and all the other revolutionary leaders lived in caves carved into the mountainside. They had little to offer other than a vision for a new China – but that, along with their charisma and conviction, was enough to attract young people from around the country, including many artists and musicians like Li. For this reason, and because culture played a crucial propaganda role in the Communist cause, Yan'an had a vibrant cultural life that included the Lu Xun Academy for Arts and Literature, poetry societies, drama groups and publications.

Xian Xinghai – who had argued that Beethoven-like greatness could only be acquired through suffering – was one of the many artists who moved to Yan'an. There, under the most challenging of circumstances, he composed the 'Yellow River Cantata', a choral work that became an instant classic and led Mao to dub him 'the people's composer'. (Unfortunately, Xian was taken ill while working in the USSR in 1945; he died in a Moscow hospital, penning a '35-year plan' for his future musical activity on his deathbed.)

At the request of Zhou Enlai, Li Delun and the composer He Luting recruited some young farm boys to establish an orchestra. 'These kids had never even seen a Western instrument in their dreams!' Li told us. 'I was a graduate of the Shanghai Conservatory, but I had to start with the piccolo and go all the way to the tuba, teaching them how to play!'

sts at Yan'an had widely varying backgrounds, coming from Communist-controlled areas ..... from Nationalist zones. There was no penalty for this – indeed, He Luting himself had worked in the wartime capital of Chongqing with the composer Ma Sicong to found the Zhonghua Orchestra, the first all-Chinese professional symphony. It received financial support from the USSR and played Beethoven's Third, Fifth and Sixth symphonies; in 1944 the United States' Vice-President Henry Wallace visited Chongqing and brought some scores with him. In 1946 the Zhonghua travelled to Kunming and performed Beethoven's Fifth and Sixth for the Allied (mainly American) forces based in the city. (A recording of the concerts was made and subsequently sent to the United States and made into a record; President Franklin D. Roosevelt reportedly got a copy and presented it to Madame Soong Mei-ling, Chiang Kai-shek's wife, who then gave it to China's central radio station.)

Mao felt it necessary to get all these different people on the same political page, so in 1942 he gave a series of formative speeches that became known as the 'Talks at the Yan'an Forum on Arts and Literature'. He spoke out-doors, beneath a bright moon and glittering stars, sharing his ideas about the future of the arts in a Communist China. A 'cultural army', he told the assembled crowd, was 'absolutely indispensable for uniting our own ranks and defeating the enemy'. But if it was to succeed, its members had to understand that literature and art should be created for the workers, peasants, soldiers and urban petty bourgeoisie who formed 90 per cent of the population – not for the bourgeois intellectuals and other exploiting classes.

Mao asked whether it was more important to raise artistic standards or put resources towards popularisation – and then answered his own question: popularisation came first, standards second. Artists had to come down from their ivory towers and learn from the masses; they should make art that ordinary people can understand, and spread it far and wide. 'In the world today,' Mao said, 'all literature and art belong to definite classes and are geared to definite political lines. There is in fact no such thing as art for art's sake, art that stands above classes or art that is detached from or independent of politics.'[67]

Mao's speech was the opening shot in a decades-long debate between those who felt that Beethoven and classical music were a means of reform and those who saw them as a distraction, or even a deterrent, from revolutionary goals.

These opposing visions of Beethoven were reflected in interesting ways in literature, with some writers, such as Mu Shiying, portraying Beethoven as nothing more than a symbol of effete bourgeois sophistication. Pan

Heling, the hero of a story by Mu, is a writer with nicotine-stained fingers and neurotic friends who mingle in a house that had 'a statue of Tolstoy, a small radio . . . Pu'er tea, banana peels, cigarette butts and smoke, laughter, historical materialism, American culture, an eight-inch photo of Greta Garbo, walls of books, modernism, sofa'.[68] And when Pan is alone, yearning for his Japanese mistress, he listens to Beethoven's Minuet in G.

For the writer Guo Moruo, however, Beethoven was the source of inspiration and purpose that Fu Lei and others had hoped he would become. In the romantic poem 'By Electric Light', Guo adopts the voice of a sad and lonely urbanite wandering through an art gallery with gloom in his heart – until he comes across a portrait of Beethoven:

Ah! Beethoven! Beethoven! You dispel my nameless grief!
    Your disheveled hair streams like swiftly flowing
waves, your high white collar is like a snow-capped ridge;
your leonine forehead, your tigerish eyes, your brain
which is like 'the will of the universe' itself.
    In your right hand a pen, in your left a manuscript, an
angry torrent flows from the point of your pen.
    Beethoven! What are you listening to?
    It is as if I were hearing your symphony.[69]

In another short story, 'Red Beans' by Zong Pu, both

versions of the composer are captured in a tale in which Beethoven's music brings together two college-age lovers:

One warm spring day, Jiang Mei walked out of the studio to find Qi Hong standing outside as usual. She had been going through Beethoven's 'Moonlight Sonata,' but just could not get it right; so she had given up in frustration. Qi Hong was in an unusually amiable mood and he asked her, 'Why did you stop?'

'I can't get it right,' Jiang Mei replied, somewhat surprised.

'You're probably concentrating too hard on your fingers. Don't think too much about them, just keep your mind on the melody and you'll get it right.'

Qi Hong walks Jiang Mei home and they talk about music the entire way:

Qi Hong said, 'I adore Beethoven. Such a giant. His works are so rich but also so simple. Every note is full of poetry.'

Jiang Mei's eyes showed that she understood he meant poetry in the widest sense.

'You like Beethoven, too, don't you?' he continued.

The romance ultimately fails, however, because Jiang Mei realises 'that the exploitation of the many by the few had to be ended', and that Qi Hong, the boy who adores Beethoven, can never make her happy – only the Communist Party can do that. It is to revolution that Jiang Mei will dedicate her life, not to bourgeois pleasures such as Beethoven.

Although 'Red Beans' is fiction, the tension it expresses was very real – a time was coming when many Chinese would have to make similar choices. The debate as to whether Beethoven was a mere plaything of the bourgeoisie or a powerful inspiration for revolution would last for decades and become ever more politicised. But even as the philosophical battlelines were being drawn, the exigencies of the actual war being fought throughout China at this time required that those who supported Beethoven, and by extension classical music, lay aside their differences with those who opposed him. The two versions of Beethoven could coexist, at least for a time.

V

Leaning to One Side

Fortunately, those who loved Beethoven, and who supported conservatory-style education and the professional performance of classical music, had two important advocates on their side: the Soviet Union and its ally East Germany. The USSR was of paramount importance to China in the first decade following the establishment of the People's Republic. Even before the Communist victory, Mao famously stated that China 'must lean to one side'.[70] He added, 'We belong to the side of the anti-imperialist front headed by the Soviet Union, and so we can turn only to this side for genuine and friendly help, not to the side of the imperialist front.'[71]

The USSR became China's 'dearest elder brother' and 'great teacher', whose friendship with the PRC would remain 'ten thousand years fresh and forever green'. The Soviet 'big brother' did many things to assist its 'little brother', among them sending approximately 10 000 advisers to help China with everything from building railroads, bridges and factories to establishing conservatories, opera houses and orchestras. Soviet advisors were instrumental in setting up China's entire musical infrastructure – and they brought with them an abiding love for Beethoven which had started with Comrade Lenin himself.

Lenin's Passion

Vladimir Lenin (1870–1924) was a mythic figure in the early years of the PRC. Chinese children grew up hearing stories about him much as Americans learned about George Washington. The tale of what might be called Lenin's cherry-tree moment, when he broke a vase at his aunt's house but refused to admit it, was especially popular. His mother, Maria Alexandrovna, scolded him – 'Oh, maybe the vase jumped to the floor itself!' – but still little Vladimir denied it. Back home, however, he owned up and wrote a confession. His aunt replied, 'When you make a mistake and admit it, that's an honest child' – and, as Chinese children were taught, Lenin never lied again and grew up to be pure and honest. In the 1950s, 'Lenin coats' – double-breasted, belted jackets with open collars – were all the rage, and the Soviet movie *Lenin in 1918* was so popular that many people memorised it.

Because Lenin was such an important figure in China, his taste in music also mattered – and Lenin had a thing for Beethoven.

Lenin grew up in a musical household and played the piano as a child, and he was passionate about classical music for his entire life.[72] During the early years of their marriage, Lenin and his wife, Nadya Krupskaya, often attended concerts. One of their close friends was Inessa Armand, a beautiful and accomplished revolutionary; some claim she was also Lenin's lover. Lenin would often ask Armand to play Beethoven's 'Pathetique'.[73] Once, according to a letter written by Nadya, the three went to hear a Beethoven quartet in Krakow. 'We even clubbed together to buy a season ticket,' Nadya explained, 'but for some reason the music made us terribly miserable, although an acquaintance of ours [Armand], an excellent musician, was in ecstasies over it.'[74]

Lenin's misery on hearing Beethoven was not unusual. 'Lenin was a great music lover,' wrote his friend Anatoly Lunacharsky, the USSR's first Commissar of Education, but music also 'distressed' him.[75] The writer Maxim Gorky provided some insight as to why, recounting an evening in 1920 when he and Lenin went to hear the famous Russian Jewish pianist and conductor Issay Dobrowen play Beethoven in a private residence. The artist Dmitriy Nalbandyan depicted the scene, a comfortably appointed parlour. Dobrowen plays a grand piano with its lid raised; only his left hand is visible, and there is no music on the stand. The light outside the bay windows is cold and blue, and the atmosphere in the room is concentrated. Gorky and the host, Yekaterina Peshkova, are on opposite sides of a table covered in a patterned blue cloth; Lenin sits across from them on a straight-backed chair, legs crossed and head in hand, seeming to listen pensively, with equal parts pleasure and pain.

When the sonata ended, Gorky explained, Lenin said:

'I know of nothing better than the Appassionata and could listen to it every day. What astonishing, superhuman music! It always makes me proud, perhaps naively so, to think that people can work such miracles!'

Wrinkling up his eyes, he smiled rather sadly, adding:

'But I can't listen to music very often, it affects my nerves. I want to say sweet, silly things and pat the heads of people who, living in a filthy hell, can create such beauty. One can't pat anyone on the head nowadays, they might bite your hand off. They ought to be beaten on the head, beaten mercilessly, although ideally we are against doing any violence to people. Hm – what a hellishly difficult job!'[76]

In other words, Gorky seems to say, Beethoven's music

so moved Lenin that it made him compassionate – an emotion a revolutionary could not afford to indulge.

However, if Lenin generally denied himself the pleasure of Beethoven, he did not enforce the same sacrifice on his country: the composer played a major role in Soviet culture. Beethoven had already become, in the words of the scholar Leon Botstein, 'the object of nineteenth century mythmaking as the first "free" individual artist'.[77] This image was expanded in the USSR, where Beethoven became 'the musical apotheosis of revolution'.[78] The Russian Association of Proletarian Musicians – renowned for its symphony of factory whistles[79] – performed Beethoven, and the 'conductorless' orchestra Persimfans gave an all-Beethoven program for its debut performance.[80] One Soviet scholar even asserted that Beethoven preferred the 'Russian pronunciation' of his surname to the German, while the Commissariat of Education wished to establish the USSR as Beethoven's 'second motherland'.[81] The 1927 centenary of Beethoven's death, which coincided with the tenth anniversary of the October Revolution, was widely celebrated and drew enthusiastic participation from musical factions which generally disagreed with one another.

The Soviet cultural environment constricted as the years went on, but Beethoven maintained his status as a revolutionary hero. So when Soviet advisers helped the PRC establish its new musical education and performance system, they reinforced China's pre-existing appreciation of Beethoven and made it politically acceptable under Communism. Chinese musicians and intellectuals who wanted to maintain and expand Beethoven's position in the PRC's musical world were thus able to adapt to, and promote, the socialist interpretation of the composer and his music. To help foster this new image of Beethoven, scholarship and propaganda from Soviet bloc countries was translated and published through most of the 1950s, with a special emphasis on that from East Germany.

A Socialist Beethoven for China

The first article devoted exclusively to Beethoven and published in the PRC was a 1953 translation of a speech given by East German president Wilhelm Pieck in 1952 on the 125th anniversary of Beethoven's death.[82] Pieck portrayed Beethoven as a fearless fighter who never bowed before reactionary forces. In praising Beethoven's music, Pieck focused on the Ninth Symphony, pointing out that the 'Ode to Joy' had been performed in the USSR to celebrate the 1936 'Stalin constitution', and asserting that it should be played wherever people struggled for peace. In 1955 a translation of an article by the East German academic Karl

Schoenewolf was published, in which it was argued that Beethoven's ultimate wish was to 'serve the people'; since it was only in socialist countries that his music could truly be understood by the people, Schoenewolf claimed, socialism had effectively fulfilled Beethoven's last wish.[83]

Some Chinese commentators began to write in a similar vein. One was the dramatist Sha Kefu, who reviewed a Moscow performance of *Fidelio* in 1955 and noted that Beethoven's music reflected revolutionary ideas, democracy and humanity, which is why it was so beloved by Lenin and Friedrich Engels. Sha repeated Gorky's 'Appassionata' anecdote, and added that Engels was especially fond of the Third and Fifth symphonies. (Indeed, Engels called these his 'favourite pieces of music'; after hearing both in 1841, he wrote to his sister: 'Last night's was such a concert! If you don't know this splendid piece [the Fifth], you have never heard anything like it in your life.')[84] He concluded by advising Chinese composers to study Beethoven so that they, too, could reflect reality in their music.[85]

With so much assistance and influence from the Soviet Union and East Germany, classical music flourished and Beethoven became increasingly well known. Many Chinese went to the USSR for training, including Li Delun, who enrolled at the Moscow Conservatory.

For his audition to study under the Moscow State Symphony conductor Nikolai Anosov, Li conducted the first movement of Beethoven's First.

Performances of Beethoven's music in China increased. The newly established Central Philharmonic debuted in October 1956, with an East German conductor, Werner Gosling, leading two all-Beethoven programs that included the Egmont Overture, incidental music inspired by Goethe's tale of a heroic Dutch nobleman who is executed for fighting against oppression, the First Piano Concerto and the Sixth Symphony, known as the 'Pastoral', which Beethoven described as 'a recollection of country life. More an expression of feeling than a painting.'[86]

In April 1957 Ma Sicong commemorated the 130th anniversary of Beethoven's death with a concert that included the Fifth Symphony and the violin Romance in F Major. More than a thousand people attended, and Gosling gave a talk with the title 'Beethoven's Spirit Has Made All Progressive People Join Together'.[87] David Oistrakh toured China later that year and played Beethoven's Violin Concerto in D Major with the Central Experimental Opera Orchestra under the baton of Li Guoquan; he also gave a private concert at the Soviet embassy, which was attended by Chairman Mao and the entire Communist Party politburo.

With Soviet encouragement, China began sending young pianists to compete in international competitions. Liu Shikun – who could hum complete Beethoven symphonies at the age of five – took third place in the 1956 Liszt Festival and second place in the 1958 Tchaikovsky Festival, just behind Van Cliburn. Yin Chengzong tied for second place at the 1962 Tchaikovsky Competition, behind first place winners Vladimir Ashkenazy and John Ogdon. Fu Lei's son Fou Ts'ong qualified for the 1955 Chopin Competition, delighting his proud father, who declared that while he himself was 'a tool for morality and art', his son was 'a brilliant artist'.[88] Before Fou Ts'ong left for Poland, the proud Fu Lei told his son, 'You must first of all be a man, then an artist, then a musician, and lastly a pianist.' When Fou Ts'ong came back from Warsaw a winner, he was for a time accorded near celebrity status.

Capitalist Beethoven vs Socialist Beethoven

The creation of a socialist Beethoven did not end the political debates that had surrounded the composer, and classical music, since before liberation. By the mid-1950s political movements were increasingly frequent, schizophrenic and harsh. In the 1956 Hundred Flowers campaign, for example, intellectuals were encouraged to speak their minds and even offer criticisms of the

Communist Party's rule; in the 1957 Anti-Rightist Campaign, many of the people who had spoken out were arrested for doing so. Fu Lei was among the 300 000 intellectuals who were denounced, demoted or exiled, as was the author Zong Pu. (Fou Ts'ong had gone back to Eastern Europe to study; after his father was declared a rightist, he went to London, where he married Zamira Menuhin, daughter of the renowned violinist Yehudi Menuhin.)

The political divisions of this era were portrayed by Shanghai Conservatory composer Mao Yurun, who described a mass meeting at which musicians were lectured on the class orientation of all human activity and the superiority of the proletariat. One attendee asked how it was possible to distinguish the 'class character' of two versions of Beethoven's Violin Concerto, one by Jascha Heifetz, who trained in the capitalist United States, and another by Oistrakh, who trained in the socialist USSR. The packed assembly hall fell silent – and then filled with snickering and whispers, since the musicians all knew the question was unanswerable. Furious, the Communist Party cadre leading the meeting denounced the questioner as 'an out and out alien-class element'.[89]

At the Shanghai Symphony, a timpanist and conductor named Lu Hongen objected to the increasing political control over the arts, arguing that the music director should be the leader of the orchestra, not the

Communist Party representative. During a required study session of Mao's Yan'an talks, Lu responded to criticism of Beethoven by querying rhetorically, 'Should Beethoven look up to the workers, peasants and soldiers or should the workers, peasants and soldiers look up to Beethoven? I think the latter. The workers, peasants and soldiers should raise their artistic cultivation.'[90]

Even as these movements and arguments were being waged, a new economic and social campaign was underway: the tragically (some would say criminally) misguided Great Leap Forward. The slogan of the Great Leap was 'more, better, cheaper, faster', and its original goal was drastically increased steel output and agricultural production. But the fervour soon spilled over into all other areas of social and economic endeavour, including music. To demonstrate their patriotism, the leaders of the Central Philharmonic felt obliged to increase the number of concerts they performed from forty to eighty. That figure was soon deemed too meagre, so they repeatedly doubled it until they settled on the absurd number of 1200 performances per year.[91] Mao Yurun explained that musicians were also expected to compose more, better and faster:

Musically during the 'Great Leap Forward' we musicians were urged to create greater pieces than those written by the great masters of the 19th century in the western world. We were indoctrinated with the belief that 'Mozart is nothing, Beethoven is nothing; they all belonged to the past ages, having nothing in common with the great proletarian masses!'[92]

Shanghai Symphony Orchestra conductor Lu Hongen

While the leftists might have condemned Beethoven as 'nothing', they still regarded his symphonies as the gold standard and asked composers to 'create something far greater than Beethoven's Ninth Symphony' – in one week. Unsurprisingly, the symphony on which Mao Yurun and his colleagues laboured for five sleepless days and nights 'went into a wastebasket'. The entire Great Leap Forward also proved to be a failure, resulting in a devastating famine in which an estimated 25 million people starved to death.

The Ninth and the Tenth

The madness of the Great Leap was temporarily suspended in 1959 – at least in music circles – to allow commemorations of the tenth anniversary of the founding of the PRC, an event of unparalleled significance to the young nation's revolutionary leaders. To celebrate, the Musicians Association decided to present the country with a gift: Beethoven's Ninth Symphony, performed for the first time by an all-Chinese orchestra and sung by an all-Chinese chorus – in Chinese.[93] Because it was also the tenth anniversary of the German Democratic Republic (East Germany), the Dresden Philharmonic would visit China later that year, and it, too, would perform Beethoven for joint celebrations of the shared anniversary.

In accordance with the spirit of the Great Leap, Central Philharmonic leader Li Ling framed the performance of the Ninth as an arduous undertaking that would involve struggle, difficulty and bitterness. By working together night and day, however, the orchestra members would surmount this pinnacle of world art and achieve victory and joy.[94] Because this was the era of 'mass line' politics, all decisions were supposed to be made by inclusive committees of 'the masses' – not, in the case of an orchestra, by an all-powerful conductor. Accordingly, an 'instrument group' was created and given the authority to determine bowings and phrasings, while Li Delun was obliged to form a 'conductors group' with choral conductor Yan Liangkun and several assistants. Sometimes the musicians would summon the conductors on short notice and demand to rehearse a particular section of the music simply to emphasise that the masses were in charge. They would remind the maestros: 'The masses walk in front, the conductor walks behind.'

Because of the Great Leap, most of the Central Philharmonic's musicians and choristers were out in the countryside teaching poetry and songs to farmers and giving small concerts to meet their outlandish performance goal. They were thrilled when Li Ling called them back to Beijing for a 'Beethoven study month', during which they read books, attended lectures and

The Central Philharmonic performing Beethoven's Ninth, 1959

art exhibitions, listened to various Beethoven recordings and had long discussions. Rehearsals then began, and continued virtually nonstop for three months, with the goal of ensuring that every musician knew the symphony inside out. To better prepare, the orchestra resumed giving regular concerts, which had largely ceased with the Great Leap; Yan Liangkun programmed Beethoven's Third at almost every one.

Anticipation for the 4 July premiere of the Ninth at Beijing's Capital Theatre was so great that tickets sold out within minutes; Central Conservatory president Ma Sicong recalled a long line snaking outside the box office, the lucky people clutching blue tickets as they departed.[95] Because demand was so high, nearly a dozen performances were added, allowing 25 000 people to hear it – including Premier Zhou Enlai and Foreign Minister Chen Yi, with the East German ambassador as their guest.

When the 1 October anniversary arrived, foreign dignitaries from socialist nations filled Beijing for the start of a three-day holiday full of parades, performances and other festivities. These included, on 3 October, a concert attended by both Mao and the Soviet First Secretary Nikita Khrushchev that included a 300-piece orchestra conducted by Li Delun playing two overtures: Li Huanzhi's Spring Festival and Beethoven's Egmont.[96] Beethoven had reached a revolutionary pinnacle in the

PRC, being now considered 'socialist' enough for Mao himself.

The Dresden Philharmonic toured China throughout the month, performing Beethoven-heavy programs heard by 150 000 people in concert halls, communes and chemical plants in Xian, Chongqing, Nanjing and Shanghai.[97] In Beijing the orchestra shared the stage with the nineteen-year-old pianist Liu Shikun, whose triumphant performance of the 'Emperor' Concerto was hailed as 'a recognition that Western classical music has come of age in New China'.[98]

The highpoint of the visit came with two further performances of the Ninth. On 11 October the Dresden Philharmonic and the Central Philharmonic Chorus joined forces to perform it under the baton of Dresden conductor Heinz Bongartz. The *Peking Review* sounded somewhat weary in its review. 'The "Choral" is no novelty to Peking audiences,' it said. 'Since last July, the Central Philharmonic Symphony Orchestra and Chorus has performed it a number of times.'[99] However, it continued, the joint performance was of 'a higher order' than others, and provided a 'moving scene' when the 'silver-haired' Bongartz hugged the young Yan Liangkun.

Later in the month, the Dresden orchestra returned to Beijing for a final performance of the Ninth in a unique venue: the 10 000-seat auditorium of the new Great Hall of the People, which had been built by volunteers during the Great Leap Forward in just ten months. The consecration of the new seat of the PRC government with a performance of Beethoven's Ninth was a momentous undertaking, so the Dresden orchestra joined forces with the Central Philharmonic, doubling its size. Choruses from the Central Conservatory and Central Broadcasting Orchestra were also invited, bringing the total number of people on stage to 330. Bongartz conducted the first three movements, and then handed his baton to Yan Liangkun, who led the final 'Ode to Joy' movement.[100]

Writing in the *Peking Daily*, Li Guoquan praised Bongartz and declared that the Ninth 'inspires audiences to the highest lofty ideals of mankind, namely peace, unity and love to all the peoples of the world'.[101] The *People's Daily*, meanwhile, proclaimed that Beethoven's dream of 'universal brotherhood' was gradually being achieved, and the evidence of this was the performance of his Ninth Symphony in China.[102]

VI

Dark Night of the Soul

Sadly, the universal brotherhood whose swift arrival the *People's Daily* had optimistically predicted in the wake of the 1959 performances of Beethoven's Ninth proved short-lived. Indeed, within months of the anniversary celebrations, China's relationship with the USSR reached breaking point. Tensions had existed since 1956, when Khrushchev denounced Stalin to a closed session of the USSR's Communist Party – an action Mao saw as a betrayal of Stalin, Communism and him personally (since he hadn't been informed in advance). In 1960 the Soviet Union took the drastic step of recalling all its advisers from China. Henceforth, China no longer learned from its 'big brother' but denounced the 'Soviet revisionists'. This rift deprived China's classical music world of the protective umbrella of Soviet (and East German) support, which would come to have a tremendous impact on its development.

Old Bei

In 1963 Frederick Page, a musician from New Zealand, spent several weeks touring China's conservatories and observing its musical life.[103] He reported that Western music was widely played and China's musicians were doing well: 'They have medical care, dress allowance, instruments are provided, [and] pay is twice that of a steel-worker.' The conservatories were 'on an immense scale', and the teaching was 'deeply impressive'; students learned not only how to play their instruments, but also how to build and repair them. The Shanghai Symphony, Page explained, gave 'concerts in Shanghai, in factories, in army headquarters, in the countryside, in the satellite towns; they make recordings, work in film studios, teach.'

But Page also observed the heavy hand of politics hanging over all this musical activity:

> Behind all this stands the State. The State follows the strict Marxist line, or rather the precepts laid down by Mao at the Yan'an Conference on the Arts in 1942. Music is for people, and people are 'workers, peasants, and soldiers.' Music will draw inspiration from them,

81

it will in return inspire and encourage them. From the heart it comes, to the heart it must go. Bach is good, because of the chorales; Beethoven is good because he is a revolutionary and consciously addressing 'the people' . . . Musicians must not think themselves creatures apart. They must know sweat and toil, what it is to help build a dam, to lend a hand with the harvest, even if it is only to sing to the workers.

The 'strict line' was in fact becoming stricter even as Page toured China's conservatories. With the Soviet Union out of the picture, those leftists who had never liked Beethoven or classical music were gradually able to gain the upper hand. In May 1963 a leading leftist critic in Shanghai named Yao Wenyuan criticised Claude Debussy in the pages of a major paper for his 'impressionism' and his alleged failure to reflect the 'real' lives of the people. When the French journalist Robert Guillain visited China in 1964, just a year after Page, the situation had changed markedly:

More than ever today [the Chinese] spurn all Western thought and culture. A veritable campaign against Western literature, art, and music has raged in China since 1963, with attacks on even the most widely recognized figures, from Shakespeare to Balzac, from Beethoven to Debussy; they are all represented as part of a rotten culture, which can have corrupting effects on the Chinese.[104]

Those who viewed Beethoven as bourgeois and undesirable grew stronger, while those who defended him, and all classical music, grew weaker. Men like Yao Wenyuan began to wield more power; indeed, the strength of Yao's acidic pen was such that the public performance of classical music ceased for an entire decade following his anti-Debussy polemic. As fear and uncertainty spread, some unknown person at the Shanghai Symphony wrote brief political evaluations of all the works in its repertoire. Analysing Beethoven's symphonies, he wrote that the Third advocated 'individualistic heroism', the Fifth was nicknamed 'Fate', and the Sixth advocated 'the leisure life of the well-off class'.[105]

In the early months of 1966, Mao Zedong's wife, Jiang Qing, began to work as a cultural advisor to the People's Liberation Army; joining forces with Yao Wenyuan and two other hardcore leftists, she formed a group that became known as the Gang of Four. Jiang Qing announced that China's cultural world was in the midst of a sharp struggle: ever since 1949, her husband's correct policies had been thwarted by the dictatorship of sinister anti-Party elements, people who followed an anti-socialist black line and favoured art that was bourgeois or revisionist, or that dated to the semi-colonial era of the 1930s. Jiang Qing did not mention Beethoven by name, but 'Old Bei', as he became known, was certainly in this category. In May the newspapers officially proclaimed the start of the 'Great Socialist Cultural Revolution'. Mao declared that 'rebellion is justified', and gangs of teenaged Red Guards marched through the streets, seeking to destroy any remnants of the 'Four Olds' – old customs, culture, habits and ideas.

In September 1966 the prominent UK-based academic Isaac Deutscher, a biographer of Stalin and Leon Trotsky, gave an interview to the Italian Communist journal *La Sinistra*, in which he analysed the situation in China:

Naturally, the old intelligentsia have had relatively close ties with Western as well as with their own native cultural traditions. For many of them, Shakespeare and Beethoven and the great figures of French literature are part of a cherished heritage . . . Now you have a reaction against all this. In the name of Marxism-Leninism, Shakespeare, Beethoven, Balzac are denounced as a specimen of bourgeois degeneration. The great 'revolutionaries' that denounce them do not even suspect – or do they? – that Karl Marx had a lifelong admiration for Balzac and Shakespeare, that Lenin loved Beethoven and Pushkin (Pushkin's monument, erected in Shanghai after the revolution, has been defaced!) . . . When they throw

Shakespeare and Beethoven into the dustbin, they may imagine that they are acting in an 'egalitarian' spirit; but this is reactionary, not progressive.

Whether or not the prevailing attitude in the PRC was reactionary or progressive, the 'old intelligentsia' who had devoted their lives to promoting Beethoven and classical music would suffer horrendously during the brutal opening years of the Cultural Revolution. Their stories stand as a tragic and enduring testament to their heroism in the face of the tremendous upheavals that they, and many others, experienced throughout this dark period.

Heroic Souls

Tan Shuzhen, the violinist who played Beethoven's Fifth with the Shanghai Symphony for the 1927 Beethoven centenary, was accused of 'dressing like a Westerner' and locked up in a closet beneath the stairs at the Conservatory for nine months. When he was finally released, he was put to work repairing the Conservatory's 122 toilets. 'I just thought of my family,' Tan said. 'I wanted to see them again . . . I never thought to commit suicide because I'm a Christian. I just thought, "The sun will come out. It's night, but the sun will come out, eventually."'[106]

Li Cuizhen, the pianist who entered the Shanghai

Conservatory able to play all thirty-two Beethoven piano sonatas, was made to crawl on the ground and call herself names while Red Guards poured ink over her head. One night she put on her best clothes and makeup, wrote a note – 'I need a rest' – and turned on the gas.

The conductor Li Guoquan was beaten severely; Red Guards also shaved one side of his head, the 'yin-yang' haircut used to humiliate 'counter-revolutionaries'. He killed himself on 26 August 1966.

Ma Sicong, the composer and Central Conservatory president, was imprisoned in a building that had once been used for piano storage. He was dragged out daily for abuse; Red Guards beat him with metal belt buckles, made him crawl on the floor like an animal and paraded him in front of former students, who spat at him and called him names. He ultimately escaped, fleeing to Hong Kong and then obtaining CIA assistance to resettle in the United States. His family members who remained in China were persecuted mercilessly.

Liu Shikun, who had played Beethoven's 'Emperor' Concerto with the Dresden Philharmonic, was imprisoned and beaten so badly that a bone in his right forearm cracked; he later told *People* magazine that the hardest part of his ordeal was 'being without a piano for six years in isolated confinement in the company of only prison guards'.[107] To pass the time, he said, 'I kept practicing music in my head and I even composed a concerto –

though I had no pen or paper to write it down.'

Fu Lei was at home with Zhu Meifu on 30 August 1966 when Red Guards from the local housing bureau stormed their house; later that night they were replaced by Red Guards from the Shanghai Conservatory. For four days and three nights, these Red Guards turned the house upside down – even digging up the rose garden and pulling up the floorboards – in search of 'evidence' of Fu's 'counter-revolutionary' crimes. Finally they found an old trunk that Fu was storing for an elderly relative; it contained a mirror, the backing of which held a pre-war photo of Chiang Kai-shek, and this became 'proof' of Fu's anti-Party crimes. When Fu and Zhu refused to expose the trunk's owner, the Red Guards crowned the couple

Fu Lei

with dunce caps and dragged them in front of a mob.[108]

Fu and Zhu had not seen their son Fou Ts'ong since Fu was branded a rightist, but Zhou Enlai had given them special permission to correspond. Just a few weeks before their arrest, on 12 August, Fu had written a letter to his daughter-in-law expressing delight in his grandson, who was about to turn two, but adding: 'I see no hope at all to meet him one day, to embrace him, taking him in my arms . . . Mamma does believe in this possibility, but not I.'[109] He had added, 'Life is hard everywhere, we have to "reform" ourselves constantly, struggling against every bit of traditional, capitalistic, non-Marxist thinking and sentiments and customs . . . For a person who lived more than 40 years in the old society . . . Mao's "self-reform" is of course a tremendously difficult task.'

Three weeks later Fu went into his study to put his affairs in order. Picking up his writing brush for the final time, he dipped it in ink and wrote an apologetic but detailed note to his brother-in-law, asking him to settle certain affairs, such as the return of items borrowed from friends, and payment of the rent and the housekeeper's wages (for which he left money). At the end of the note, he wrote the date – 'Night of 2 September 1966' – and placed his seal. Then he and Zhu went to their bedroom and hanged themselves from the metal grill doorframes; they used lengths of cotton cloth handwoven in Fu's home town, Pudong.

Lu Hongen, the outspoken conductor of the Shanghai Symphony, was forced to participate in discussions of Yao Wenyuan's criticism of three well-known intellectuals who wrote under the pseudonym 'Three Family Village'. Yao had labelled the threesome – Deng Tuo, Wu Han and Liao Mosha – 'anti-Party', and Lu was supposed to parrot the charge. When he refused, he was thrown in jail, where he became Prisoner 1144.[110]

Prisoners were also obliged to participate in mandatory criticism sessions, and now Lu was asked to condemn the composer He Luting, who had become president of the Shanghai Conservatory and was also being persecuted horribly. Unsurprisingly, Lu refused to criticise his former teacher; instead, he praised him as a master musician. He did, however, criticise Jiang Qing, saying, 'I'd rather be a counter-revolutionary than a part of the "big revolution" orchestrated by that witch.'

Incidents such as these were followed by severe beatings and abuse; on one occasion the guards dumped Lu's food on the ground and made him eat like a dog. Lu, a Catholic, coped, according to his fellow prisoner Liu Wenzhong, by humming his two favourite Beethoven pieces, the Third Symphony and the 'Missa Solemnis'. Of the latter piece Beethoven had once said, 'My chief aim was to awaken and permanently instil religious feelings not only into the singers but also into the listeners.'[111]

The more Lu talked, the more abuse was heaped on him. Liu urged him to keep quiet, for the sake of his son, but it was to no avail. The mistreatment seems to have gradually eroded Lu's reason, if not his spirit; whenever he saw an object that was red or made of wool (a homonym for Mao), he would frantically try to tear it apart.

On one occasion he shredded a copy of the 'Little Red Book' of Chairman Mao's sayings. This was an unimaginable blasphemy and led to a special criticism session, at which a guard shouted, 'Prisoner 1144, do you want to live or die?'

Lu thought for several minutes. 'I want to live,' he replied at last. 'But I don't want to live like the walking dead – without freedom, I'd rather die . . . The Cultural Revolution has destroyed truth, friendship, love, happiness, peace and security and hope . . .' He went on in this vein for some time before the shocked guards trundled him away.

Back in his cell, the beaten and bloodied Lu spoke urgently with his friend Liu. 'If you get out,' Lu said, 'I ask you two things. The first is to help me find my son, who has been sent to Xinjiang; tell him how his father died in jail. The second, if you ever have a chance to escape China, is to help me do something I have wanted to do my entire life. Visit Austria, the home of music. Go to Beethoven's tomb and lay a bouquet of flowers. And tell Beethoven that his disciple in China, Lu Hongen, was humming the 'Missa Solemnis' as he march death.'

A week later, at midnight, Lu was called out of his cell. He left, as promised, humming the 'Missa Solemnis', through lips cracked from beatings. On 27 April 1968 he was taken to Shanghai Culture Square and paraded before a mass rally that was broadcast live on Shanghai television. The crowd of 10 000 sang 'Sailing the Seas with the Great Helmsman', a paean to Mao, and applauded and shouted slogans when it was announced that Lu and six other 'counter-revolutionaries' would be executed. Lu was put in the back of a truck and driven to the killing ground. His vocal cords were slit so he couldn't shout anything in the moment before he died, and then he was shot. A bill for the bullet was delivered to his mother, who was too afraid to collect her son's body.

Beethoven's life and music had given meaning and purpose to the lives of these men and women, inspiring and sustaining them for decades – but it could not save them from the vicious political insanity of the Cultural Revolution. We can only hope that each of these heroic souls was somehow sustained by the implicit promise of Beethoven, as expressed by Romain Rolland:

[Beethoven] is the heroic energy of modern art, the greatest and best friend of all who suffer and struggle. When we mourn over the sorrows of the world, he comes to our solace. It is as if he seated himself at the piano in the room of a bereaved mother, comforting her with the wordless song of resignation . . . What . . . can compare in refulgence with this superhuman effort, this triumph of the spirit, achieved by a poor and unhappy man, by a lonely invalid, by one who, though he was sorrow incarnate, though life denied him joy, was able to create joy that he might bestow it on the world. As he himself proudly phrases it, he forges joy out of his own misfortunes . . . The device of every heroic soul must be: 'Out of suffering cometh joy.'[112]

VII

Triumph of the Spirit

Beethoven's Chinese disciples had promoted his music and curated his image for decades. They had adapted it for survival under socialism. Some had paid for their efforts with their lives. But if Beethoven was down, felled by the dual blows of the Sino-Soviet split and the Cultural Revolution, he was never out: the private, personal Beethoven, beloved of so many in China, could never be crushed. The public Beethoven, both sage and revolutionary, who had been woven into China's political culture, would inevitably return.

Hidden Beethoven

During the Cultural Revolution, public culture was dominated by the 'model revolutionary operas' that were created under Jiang Qing's guidance. These 'operas' – which included reformed Peking operas, ballets, a symphony and a piano concerto – were performed on every stage in the nation, adapted to film and broadcast ad nauseam over radio and TV. Schoolchildren competed to perform in them; to this day, many people who lived through that era can sing every word of every opera.

In the privacy of their homes, however, it was not uncommon for people to listen to Beethoven. Guo Jianying, the son of the poet Guo Moruo, recalled listening over and over to a recording of Liu Shikun performing the 'Emperor' Concerto with the Dresden Philharmonic. Many people also filled long hours by reading Fu Lei's translation of *Jean-Christophe*. Some read the novel and listened to Beethoven at the same time; the scholar Barbara Mittler quotes one unnamed university professor who described doing just that:

At home, with all these girls' and boys' parents gone to labor camp, we would meet all the time. We would read things like (Romain Rolland's) *Jean-Christophe* and listen to music by Beethoven. Everybody would do that. Really, *Jean-Christophe* was one of the most popular novels all that time. And what we did was somehow like group education, the books just moved on from one person to the next and then became a topic of conversation, and we would develop these collective fantasies about writing great novels ourselves. Music actually always accompanied these readings. Of course, it was not allowed and I seem to remember that all of these books that we passed round had a kind of paper cover. I was 13 then, I knew and had read so little before and so for me, this whole period at the beginning of the Cultural Revolution was like a great awakening.[113]

One of the people secretly studying Beethoven during the Cultural Revolution was none other than Premier Zhou Enlai. Zhou was the architect of China's slight opening to the West, which began in 1971 with an invitation for the US table tennis team to visit Beijing. This was followed by a secret visit by US national security adviser Henry Kissinger, and then by a ground-breaking 1972 visit from President Richard Nixon.

Kissinger went to Beijing several more times. Before one of these visits, Zhou summoned Central Philharmonic conductor Li Delun and suggested that the orchestra give the visiting American a private concert. 'Premier Zhou said to me, "Kissinger's German. You should play Beethoven,"' Li said. Zhou then asked Li to explain all nine Beethoven symphonies to him, and to follow up with written materials so he could continue studying. In order to keep his Beethoven interest confidential, Zhou asked Li to leave the materials at his private office in the State Council rather than at the West Gate of the Zhongnanhai leadership compound, as was normal practice.

When Jiang Qing heard that Beethoven had been added to Kissinger's schedule, she and her close colleague Yu Huiyong called Li in. Jiang Qing first asked which Beethoven symphony the Central Philharmonic played best. The Fifth, Li told her – but Yu Huiyong objected that it was about fatalism. Li then suggested the Third, but Yu nixed that too, proclaiming it to be about Napoleon. Li decided to keep quiet after that, so Jiang Qing asked Yu for his view. He suggested that Beethoven's Sixth was acceptable since it was about nature – so that's what the Central Philharmonic had to play.[114]

Kissinger somewhat sarcastically recalled the February 1973 performance in the second volume of his memoirs.[115] The Chinese, he said, 'did us the greatest kindness imaginable' by sparing him and his colleagues 'one of the revolutionary operas whose stupefying simple-mindedness one could escape only by a discreet doze.' Instead:

They attempted – if I may use the word – the Sixth Symphony of Beethoven. Not even my affection for things Chinese can induce me to report that the Chinese musicians were in their element when attempting the

Pastoral Symphony after the destructive interruption of the Cultural Revolution; indeed, there were moments when I was not clear exactly what was being played or from which direction on the page.

Li knew they had played badly and was embarrassed; afterwards, he requested special permission from Jiang Qing to rehearse ten foreign symphonies, including Beethoven's.[116] She agreed, and also decided to learn more about the music of Beethoven and other composers herself. She asked Li to organise a tutorial – with the stipulation that it exclude Schumann and Brahms, whose music she disliked, and all compositions by bourgeois composers who lived when the bourgeoisie was rising to its peak. This meant Beethoven was acceptable, but not Tchaikovsky, Debussy or any modernists, because they were from the era of bourgeoisie decline.[117]

Although Kissinger criticised the Central Philharmonic's rendering of the Sixth, he also recognised that the symbolism of their playing Beethoven was more significant than the execution. Zhou Enlai, he wrote, 'intended to modernize, that is, to throw off the shackles of China's recent past and to adapt his country not only to Western technology but also to an awareness of the Western culture that had spawned it'. Mao, too, seemed ready to open China at this point:

[Mao] knew now – if perhaps only as a transient conviction – that China's continuing to live apart from the rest of the world would ensure its irrelevance and expose it to untold danger. China, he indicated not without melancholy, would have to go to school abroad. He had halted the Cultural Revolution, and he remarked with sadness that the Chinese people were 'very obstinate and conservative.' The time had come for them to study foreign languages, he said, which was another way of stressing the importance of learning from abroad. That, too, had been the symbolism of playing Beethoven at the cultural event.

Zhou's push for more openness continued after this private concert, which began an intriguing period of 'classical music diplomacy' in which Beethoven played a central role. It started with a visit by the London Philharmonic in March 1973 – they played Beethoven's exhilarating Seventh Symphony (which the composer called 'one of my best works') and other works during two packed performances at the Tianqiao Theatre. The 22 March edition of the *People's Daily* covered the performances in an article headlined 'Excellent Music Performance, Fresh Artistic Style'.[118] Next came the Vienna Philharmonic, under Claudio Abbado; it played Beethoven's Third Symphony (even though Yu Huiyong had not permitted the Central Philharmonic to play it).

Following the Nixon visit, the United S[...] China agreed to exchange cultural delega[...] Americans would begin by sending to Beijing scholars, scientists and athletes – and the renowned Philadelphia Orchestra. The orchestra's visit was scheduled for September 1973. The Americans attempted to finalise logistical details, including the number of concerts, the cities in which they would play, and what would be on the program. But according to Frank Tenny, a State Department official closely involved in the arrangements, for six months there was no reply.[119]

The orchestra's renowned conductor, Eugene Ormandy, grew anxious – he wanted to rehearse before embarking on such an historic tour. Finally, he chose the programs himself, keeping in mind China's political restrictions, as he understood them: no Russian, baroque or romantic music. The Americans passed on Ormandy's choices, which included Beethoven's Fifth, to their Chinese interlocutors. But the only response was cryptic: 'Don't play *Don Juan*.' Presumably this was because the fictional Don Juan was a libertine.

The Philadelphia Orchestra landed in Shanghai, en route to Beijing. Nicholas Platt, the US liaison in the capital, met the orchestra members at the airport and escorted them on their final flight to the Chinese capital. Once at the hotel in Beijing, Tenny, Platt, the orchestra manager, Boris Sokoloff, and Douglas

Murray of the National Committee on US-China Relations met with a Mr Liu, from the Chinese side. They were seeking answers to many questions. Where were the concerts to be? In what cities, on what dates, at what hours, with what programs? When and what would the musicians eat?

As Tenny recalled:

Mr. Liu answered pleasantly but with the necessary minimum of details about dates, bus pick up, hours, etc. After some 15 minutes he said, 'We'd like to have you play Beethoven's Sixth Symphony.'

'Oh' Sokoloff said, 'if you had asked us earlier, we would have been delighted to prepare and play the Sixth. But the Maestro doesn't play it too often. He hasn't played it in some years, and we don't have the music with us.'

The discussion went back to logistics, but Mr Liu soon circled back to his request:

'What about Beethoven's Sixth?'

'We don't have the music, as I told you, so it is out of the question,' Sokoloff said. He did, however, send someone to waken the music librarian and ask him to join us. When the librarian arrived, Sokoloff asked him if he had brought the music for Beethoven's Sixth. 'No,' the librarian answered in surprise. 'You didn't tell me to, and you know the Maestro hasn't played it in years.'

The US side again steered the conversation back to practicalities, but to no avail:

> Another twenty minutes and Mr. Liu repeated, 'What about Beethoven's Sixth?'
>
> 'I'm sorry but it's out of the question. We don't have the scores,' Sokoloff repeated.
>
> 'But,' said Mr. Liu, 'we will loan you the scores. Our orchestras have them.'
>
> 'Thank you,' said Sokoloff, 'but we have a large orchestra and we would need at least 115 sets of parts.'
>
> 'That's all right,' said Mr. Liu. 'We have orchestras all over China and we will have the scores flown in for you tomorrow.'
>
> 'Thank you,' said Sokoloff, 'but there is no time to rehearse. The Maestro is very particular. We must rehearse so that the strings can mark the bowing.'

At four a.m. the meeting adjourned; Mr Liu's parting words were: 'We want Beethoven's Sixth.'

The only American who understood what was going on was Platt, who had been consumed by the arrangements for the tour from his base in Beijing. 'The dangers were legion,' he later wrote. 'Culture had torn China apart in recent years and Madame Mao was still in charge of culture, even with the smallest issue referred to her for decision.' He had spent endless hours 'haggling' with the Chinese Foreign Ministry and negotiating programs; his counterparts 'were petrified of the chairman's wife and the dire consequences of making a mistake', he wrote, which is why it was impossible to finalise the arrangements and programs. When he was at Shanghai airport awaiting the orchestra's arrival, he was told of the demand that they perform Beethoven's Sixth.

'Maestro Ormandy's antipathy toward Beethoven's Sixth was well known,' Platt wrote, so it was with 'trepidation' that he sat next to Ormandy on the flight to Beijing and conveyed the request. Platt explained what happened next:[120]

'You know I hate Beethoven's Sixth, and I did not even bring the scores,' [Ormandy] said.

> Talking fast, and making a lot up as I went along, I explained the authorities' peculiar predilection for the Sixth in Chinese political terms. The Chinese loved program music, and the Pastoral themes represented peasant life in the countryside. Theirs was a peasant revolution, and they identified the storm in the fourth movement with the struggle they had been through. The peaceful, triumphant final movement represented China under Communist rule. It was clear that the

Ormandy and Li Delun on the Great Wall during the Philadelphia Orchestra's historic visit in 1973

request had come from Madame Mao herself.

Ormandy sighed, and said, 'If that's what they want, that's what they shall have. I am in Rome and will do as the Romans. I will forget my own rules.' His only condition was that scores would be provided by the following afternoon. I almost collapsed with relief.

As a seasoned China hand, however, Platt did not let his Chinese counterparts know straightaway that Ormandy had agreed. He kept the development 'in his back pocket', knowing that his counterparts would try to renegotiate numerous other details of the trip, but that they 'would give us anything as long as the orchestra played the Sixth'.

In the end, Beethoven's Sixth was scheduled for 16 September, the orchestra's second Beijing performance; the US diplomats helped to copy the scores. Jiang Qing attended the concert, as did the critic and fellow Gang of Four member Yao Wenyuan; the pair sat next to Mrs Ormandy. According to Tenny, the two women 'argued' about music but stopped when the concert started.

The concert, including the under-rehearsed Sixth, went well. The *Peking Review* wrote that the orchestra's 'excellent performance won warm applause from the audience. Eugene Ormandy deeply impressed the audience by his unaffected and incisive way of conducting.'[121] Afterwards, Jiang Qing chatted with Ormandy and presented him with a gift. The musicians had already returned to their hotel, but she decided she wanted to talk to them, too, so they were all taken away from their dinner and returned to the concert hall. 'China ha[s] so much to learn about music,' she told them, 'and our music must grow from your example.'

One day the Philadelphia Orchestra members were taken to visit the Central Philharmonic. Li Delun greeted them, saying, 'We are so happy to have you come and to hear you play Beethoven. We have not played Beethoven in years, but since you are here, we would like to show you how we can.' Li then picked up his baton and led the orchestra through the first movement of Beethoven's Fifth. When it ended, he proffered his baton to a surprised Ormandy and asked him to conduct the second movement. The *New York Times* music critic described what followed:

Mr. Ormandy stood up, doffed his jacket and necktie, went to the podium and brought down his baton. The orchestra responded. It was very much in the Ormandy manner – full, resonant, singing. The Central Philharmonic sounded like a different orchestra, suddenly playing with confidence and rhythmic assurance. A glowing Mr. Ormandy paid tribute to Mr. Li for having trained so fine an orchestra.[122]

Ormandy's impromptu rehearsal of Beethoven's Fifth with the China Central Philharmonic, 1973

Maestro Li had got his revenge – the orchestra had played the Fifth, the Beethoven it knew best, for the Philadelphia Orchestra. But this victory, if sweet, was fleeting – and the pushback was fast and hard.

Before the year was out, Jiang Qing and her leftist comrades had launched a campaign against 'music without titles', or absolute music, and 'the recent weird contention that so-called absolute music has no social content but simply expresses contrasting and changing moods'. This, they said, was 'a sign of a return to the revisionist line in art and literature' that was 'reactionary and erroneous', involving 'the question of whether or not the Marxist-Leninist theory of class struggle should be recognized as a universally applicable truth'.[123] Those who believed that 'music is music, and nothing else' were 'modern revisionists'. The truth was that all music has 'class character', and Beethoven was singled out as proof of this: 'When the German bourgeois composer Beethoven . . . was asked the meaning of his Sonata No. 17, a composition without a descriptive title, he replied: "Please read Shakespeare's 'The Tempest.'" That play, we know, preaches the bourgeois theory of human nature.'

The *New York Times* covered this 'surprising' development, running a January 1974 story headlined 'China Assails Beethoven and Schubert'. It described the attacks on Beethoven and classical music, and quoted a *People's Daily* editorial bemoaning the fact that 'some people' were still 'uncritically' introducing music by Beethoven, Schubert and other classical composers to China's youth. 'If we go on like this,' the editorial asked, 'Where will our young people be led?'[124]

The question was rhetorical, the answer being apparent to the leftists who posed it: the young people would turn to Beethoven, and to the classical music of which he had become the primary representative.

VIII

Beethoven Fever

By 1975, even Mao Zedong himself seemed to have sickened of the restraints imposed by the Cultural Revolution.

> 'There are too few model plays,' he complained. 'Moreover, even the slightest mistakes are dealt with by criticism. There is no more blooming of a hundred flowers. The others cannot bring up their opinions; that's no good. There is a fear of writing articles, writing plays, novels, poems, and songs.'[125]

But Jiang Qing and her Gang of Four comrades were not ready to relinquish their grip on power. The Chinese people would be obliged to endure even more hardship before the country could return to a semblance of normality that would allow the blossoming of diverse ideas and art forms – and the performance of Beethoven.

Beethoven Rolls Over

On 8 January 1976, Zhou Enlai died, plunging much of the country into despair. To honour him, tens of thousands of people poured into Tiananmen Square on 5 April, the day of the tomb-sweeping festival. They covered every inch of every tree and bush in white mourning flowers, and stood in orderly queues to file past the Monument to the People's Heroes and paste handwritten poems onto the marble cenotaph. This demonstration of love for Zhou angered Jiang Qing and her Gang of Four comrades, who sent soldiers to clear the tributes and arrest the mourners.

On 28 July the Tangshan Earthquake struck, killing at least a quarter of a million people as they slept. Then on 9 September, Mao Zedong himself went to 'meet Marx', as the euphemism went. Fear and trepidation gripped the Chinese people as they wondered what direction their rudderless nation might take. The answer began to emerge with the 6 October arrest of the Gang of Four, which caused celebrations to erupt. Once more, tens of thousands of people marched to Tiananmen Square. Dramatic though these changes were, a climate of fear and uncertainty lingered on – social trust was in short supply, and many wondered when the leftist ideologues would return and what form their revenge would take.

It was in this atmosphere, at the beginning of 1977, that Li Delun requested permission to commemorate the 150th anniversary of Beethoven's death by playing the Fifth Symphony. Receiving no response, he rehearsed it anyway, until finally, at nine o'clock on the evening of 23 March, his phone rang.[126] The person on the other end informed him that the standing committee of the Communist Party Politburo had met to discuss his request – and permission had been granted.

A still wary *People's Daily* ran a concert announcement the next day that included titles of the Chinese works on the program but substituted 'etc.' for 'Beethoven'. Music lovers found out anyway and scrambled to get tickets, while foreign press agencies released the news: Beethoven was back.

On 26 March 1977 the Central Philharmonic took the stage in the auditorium of Beijing's Minority Nationalities Palace. A tremor of anticipation passed through orchestra and audience alike as Li walked to the podium, raised his baton, and then the famous opening notes of the Fifth filled the hall. Fate was again knocking at the door, which had reopened after so many years of suffering. The final two movements of the symphony were broadcast live on nationwide radio and television, offering proof to many that the Cultural Revolution was truly over. (The classical music critic Norman Lebrecht happened to be in Hong Kong that day and saw the broadcast – and went running down the hotel corridor and into the bar yelling, 'The Cultural Revolution's over!'[127])

Li Delun had always loved the Fifth, which, unusually, starts in C minor but ends in C major. It was especially appropriate on this occasion, since Beethoven had said: 'Many maintain that every movement in a minor key must end of necessity in the same mode. Nego. On the contrary, I find that precisely the soft scales of the major at the end have a delightful, uncommonly calming affect. Joy follows on sorrow, and sunshine on rain.'[128] The performance sparked an intense, nationwide desire to learn about, hear and play Beethoven.

'Beethoven came to assume a symbolic meaning for those who objected to the cultural restrictions imposed under the "gang of four",' the historian Timothy Brook wrote in 1979. 'The revival of Beethoven represented a new urge to recreate the common ground between Chinese and western musical culture.'[129]

Bridge to the World

In the aftermath of the Cultural Revolution, those who loved music turned again to Beethoven, using him as a bridge to the outside world and its values.

Young people flooded into the concert halls, which were filled by foreign orchestras; they returned to the conservatories, which had been shut down during the Cultural Revolution but began reopening in 1978; and they patronised the bookstores, which sprang to life as the moribund publishing industry – which for years had used virtually its entire paper quota to print Mao's works – began reissuing books about Beethoven and classical music.

In 1979 three major foreign orchestras visited China – the Toronto Symphony under Andrew Davis, the Boston Symphony under Seiji Ozawa, and the Berlin Philharmonic under Herbert von Karajan – and they all played Beethoven. The pent-up demand for music education in China was so great that the nation's overwhelmed conservatories received hundreds of thousands of applications. In 1978 alone, for instance, 18 000 people applied to the composition department at the Central Conservatory, which could only offer 100 spots. One of these would-be composers was a young man named Tan Dun, from Hunan Province.

Tan had been at work in a rice paddy several years earlier when he heard a loudspeaker broadcast of the Philadelphia Orchestra playing Beethoven. He was fascinated by the sound of the orchestra, and found Beethoven's music so 'seductive' that he instantly vowed to become 'that kind of musician'. The Central Conservatory accepted him, and eventually Tan reached the top ranks of global contemporary composers, winning an Academy Award, a Grammy Award and a Grawemeyer Award, among others.

The publishing industry began churning out Beethoven-related classics, including nearly 200000 copies of Fu Lei's translation of *Vie de Beethoven*. Fu Lei himself was 'rehabilitated' in 1979 – that is, there was an official acknowledgement that all accusations against him had been groundless – and given a memorial service. Soon after, his son Fou Ts'ong made an emotional homecoming to perform Beethoven's First and Fourth piano concertos with the Central Philharmonic under Li Delun. In 1981 the 200 letters that Fu Lei had written to his sons between 1954 and 1966 were compiled, edited and published by Fu Min. *The Fu Lei Family Letters* contained advice on how to be an artist – and a person – and invoked a humanity that had gone missing in the years of political upheaval. It sold more than a million copies and remains in print to this day.

By the 1980s Beethoven seemed to be everywhere in China. When the New Zealand musician Frederick Page returned to teach in 1981, he travelled to the ancient Silk Road city of Xi'an, where he visited the 'bleak' conservatory and heard its orchestra rehearse Beethoven's serene Fourth Symphony. He professed himself 'bowled over by the simplicity and directness of their playing: no imposing "master" reading, all fresh and spontaneous, and as moving a performance of Beethoven as I have heard'.[130]

The British conductor Jane Glover responded similarly in 1983, when she heard the Soviet-trained female conductor Zheng Xiaoying lead a sight-reading of the first movement of Beethoven's Third; Glover delighted 'at their passionate response to this music as they experienced it for the first time'.[131]

By 1984 the Central Philharmonic was able to play all nine Beethoven symphonies in one season, and in 1985 the Shanghai Symphony held a Beethoven Festival for which tickets were in such demand that people began lining up at four a.m. In 1988 Chuck Berry's 'Roll Over Beethoven' was purged from the playlist of an American pop music show that was preparing to debut on China's national radio; the broadcasting authorities had deemed it 'disrespectful' to Beethoven's memory.[132]

The travel writer Paul Theroux, who journeyed across China by train in the mid-1980s, recorded his experiences in *Riding the Iron Rooster*. In it he described an encounter with Beethoven aficionados in the remote Qinghai Province:

'What's that music?' I asked the driver, as we traveled to the hotel from the station.

The driver said nothing, but his pal said, 'Beethoven.'

'Beethoven,' the driver said. 'I like Beethoven.'

The driver's name was Mr. Fu. He said he could drive me to Tibet. It would be about five days to Lhasa, through the Qinghai desert and then into the mountains. Sleep in army camps on the way. How about it?

I said I was very interested.

Mr. Li, his pal, said, 'I think it's Symphony Number Two.'

'Isn't it Six – the *Pastorale*?'

Mr. Li laughed. He had yellow teeth. His laugh simply meant *Wrong*! It was a barklike noise. He said, 'The *Pastorale* goes dum-dum-dee-dee-dum. No, this isn't Number Two. I know Two, Five, Six, Seven and Nine. This isn't a symphony. It is an overture.'

Mr. Fu went fossicking in his glove compartment. He brought out the cassette holder and showed us. It was the *Coriolan* Overture. Mr. Fu said it was a Beethoven work he particularly liked.[133]

Beethoven again became a symbol of all that was virtuous. One visiting scholar attended a 1984 speech contest at a Shanghai university, at which a student took the stage and announced: 'Ladies and Gentlemen, I am here to talk to you about civilization, because absolutely none of you here have the tiniest inkling of what civilization means. Civilization, that is: Beethoven . . .'[134]

The capacity for repurposing Beethoven to changing

goals and circumstances remained undiminished. One Chinese scholar wrote that, in the 1980s, 'I put a typical bust of Beethoven on my table as many Chinese young people did,'[135] hoping to gain 'the powerful encouragement' of Beethoven's spirit so he could better succeed in his career. Others gave Beethoven a new political incarnation – this time as a democrat rather than a socialist. In the mid-1980s one sociologist noted that China had accepted the music of Beethoven and Mozart because it 'represented the best product of human civilization during that period'. Given this, he asked, 'Why cannot we accept other best products of human civilization during the same period, that is democracy and human rights?'[136] That question was increasingly asked, and in April 1989 protests broke out in Beijing and spread around the country, as students and workers demanded more individual freedoms and economic rights.

Tens of thousands of students occupied Tiananmen Square, and in mid-May some launched a hunger strike. In response, musicians and choristers of the Central Philharmonic loaded up their instruments and drove to Tiananmen Square to boost the spirits of the hungerstrikers – by playing Beethoven. Word of the orchestra's plan spread so quickly that more than 5000 protesters had gathered even before the instruments could be unloaded. Seated cross-legged on the ground, they waited to hear Beethoven – but the crowds ultimately made it impossible for the orchestra to set up, and in the end only the chorus could perform, singing songs like 'March of the Volunteers' and 'The Internationale'.[137]

Just a few days later, on 20 May, the government declared martial law in Beijing blasting the proclamation repeatedly through loudspeakers in Tiananmen Square. Eager to block out the ominous words, student leaders played a recording of 'Ode to Joy' over their own jerry-rigged speakers. One student leader, Feng Congde, recalled that there were 'Hundreds of thousands of students shouting as we broadcast the music on the square louder than the government system. I just had a feeling of winning, of triumph.'[138] Beethoven, Feng said, gave protesters 'a sense of hope, solidarity, for a new and better future'; the music 'transformed us'. The protests ended in tragedy, but the following year China marked the 220th anniversary of Beethoven's birth by issuing a commemorative silver coin that depicted the composer at work – writing 'Ode to Joy'.

In subsequent years, Beethoven's roots in the PRC deepened. The Ministry of Education added Romain Rolland's *Vie de Beethoven* (in a new translation) to the mandatory middle school reading list. 'Ode to Joy' was included in the definition of patriotic 'red songs' because it is 'about constant improvement'.[139] The obsession with Beethoven was even given a name: the 'Beethoven complex'.[140]

Overseas orchestras that visit China still regularly play Beethoven. In 2011 the renowned maestro Daniel Barenboim led the West-Eastern Divan Orchestra on an all-Beethoven China tour; the Vienna Philharmonic, under Christian Thielemann, visited Beijing in 2013 and gave three all-Beethoven concerts that included his First, Third, Fourth and Fifth symphonies; and when the Vienna Symphony toured China the following year, concert halls in four of the six cities visited requested that Beethoven's Third and Seventh symphonies appear on the program. Seemingly every Chinese music ensemble now wants to visit Beethoven's adopted hometown of Vienna and perform in its famous *Musikverein* – more than 130 did this in 2014 alone. Chinese visitors to Europe flock to Beethoven's birthplace of Bonn, where the *Beethoven-Haus* has added Chinese to its offering of foreign languages, along with English, French and Spanish.

China has changed immeasurably in the century and more since Li Shutong first wrote about the 'German born in Bonn' – and Beethoven has been a part of that process. The composer and his music have been woven into China's social, cultural and political fabric, and they've inspired reform, revolution and rebellion. They've given strength to the struggling, direction to the lost and solace to the suffering. Beethoven will remain a part of whatever comes next: China's sage of music.

Sheila's Epilogue

Beethoven had once declared that he would 'seize fate by the throat' and never let it overcome him. Over the tumultuous course of the twentieth century, the Chinese people did the same. They also seized Beethoven – and made him their own.

I thought of this as I stood at Beethoven's grave in Vienna's *Zentralfriedhof*, or Central Cemetery, in the summer of 2013. It was the very last stop of an extraordinary concert tour Jindong had designed and led as conductor of the Stanford Symphony Orchestra. Stanford University had been gifted a stunning concert hall by the remarkable patrons Helen and Peter Bing, and to celebrate its opening Jindong had led the orchestra in performing all nine Beethoven symphonies and all five piano concertos, followed by a concert tour in European cities important to Beethoven's development.

A dream he'd long had of performing all the Beethoven symphonies in one season had come true – and hundreds of students and thousands of audience members had shared in it.

Beethoven's grave is relatively simple: a white stone obelisk with his surname at the base, a gilt lyre surrounded by a shining sun at the centre, and at the top a butterfly encircled by a snake eating its own tail. (I later looked this up and learned that the lyre and sun symbolise Apollo, the leader of the Muses; the butterfly represents the soul; while the snake biting its own tail stands for the enduring nature of art.[141])

Death had advanced steadily on the great composer in the winter of 1826–27, hastening its steps even as Beethoven determined to keep living and creating – to finish, for instance, the Tenth Symphony that was already sketched out and in his desk. He spent his last weeks undergoing a series of operations, and was obliged to devote his final days to the prosaic task of beseeching patrons and publishers to send him financial aid. One of the last things he did was write a thank you note to the English Philharmonic Society for the funds it had recently sent in answer to his request.

Controversy surrounds the veracity of accounts detailing Beethoven's final hours, but Rolland reprints a letter penned by Beethoven's friend Anton Schindler. According to Schindler, when Beethoven finally understood the end was near, he cried, '*Plaudite, amici, comedia finita est!*' – or 'Applaud, my friends, the comedy is over!' A gift of wine and an herbal concoction reputed to cure dropsy had been sent to him, and Schindler put the wine on Beethoven's bedside table. Beethoven gazed longingly at the libation he had always loved, and said, ''Tis a pity, a pity, too late!' He then entered prolonged and evidently agonising death throes that lasted for nearly two days. At a quarter before six on the evening of 26 March 1927, Beethoven died, 'in the climax of a violent storm, a tempest of snow, heavily punctuated with terrible thunder claps'.[142]

The Stanford students had moved on to the cemetery chapel, leaving Jindong, our son and daughter and me to linger alone at the tomb. I thought of Fu Lei, and wondered if Beethoven had been able to give him any comfort in his final tortured days. I thought of Lu Hongen, and how, in 2001, his loyal former cellmate had finally been able to travel to this very spot to lay a bouquet of flowers and tell Beethoven that his 'Chinese disciple' had gone to his execution humming the 'Missa Solemnis'.

Our silent contemplation was broken by a group of middle-aged Chinese tourists bearing bouquets of flowers. They passed nearby without stopping and then circled back, as though lost. '*Bei duo fen zai nar?*' we heard one man ask no one in particular. ('Where is Beethoven?')

Hearing the question, our son ran over. '*Bei Duo Fen zai zher,*' he told them, and led them to the grave.

I watched, admiringly, as they bowed their heads and laid flowers on the tomb. They did not know enough German (or English) even to read the word *Beethoven*, yet they had ventured all the way from China to pay 'Bei Duo Fen' their respects.

China has approached Beethoven with passion – but also with purpose. The Chinese intellectuals who first introduced the composer made a decision to go out into the world, learn from it and bring back the best of Western and Japanese culture. They did it when China was weak and struggling, but determined to triumph. The ambition that led them to seek out Beethoven; the capacity of China's syncretic culture to absorb him; the flexibility with which Beethoven was adapted to changing political circumstances; the courage with which music lovers clung to Beethoven in the worst of times; and the resiliency and joy with which they resurrected him when their personal and national travails finally ended – all say much about the compelling personal story of Beethoven and the power of his music, but perhaps even more about China and its people.

Sheila Melvin
June 2015

NOTES

All web pages were accessed on 18 June 2015.

1   Geremie Barme, *An Artistic Exile: A Life of Feng Zikai (1898–1975)*, University of California Press, Berkeley & Los Angeles, 2002, p. 160.

2   David Castrillon, 'The Abolition of the Imperial Examination System and the Xinhai Revolution of 1911', *Asia Pacifico, 2012* (*http://asiapacifico.utadeo.edu.co/wp-content/uploads/2012/10/The-Abolition-of-the-Imperial-Examination-System-and-the-Xinhai-Revolution-of-1911.pdf*).

3   Barme, *An Artistic Exile*, p. 33.

4   'The Westernization of Chinese Opera', CCTV, 2008 (http://www.cctv.com/program/e_documentary/20080904/102015.shtml).

5   'The Westernization of Chinese Opera', CCTV, 2008 (http://www.cctv.com/program/e_documentary/20080904/102015_1.shtml).

6   Luciana Galliano, *Yogaku: Japanese Music in the 20th Century*, p. 96.

7   Luciana Galliano, *Yogaku: Japanese Music in the 20th Century*, p. 65.

8   Su Hsing-Lin, 'Li Shutong and the evolution of graphic arts in China', *East Asia Journal*, vol. 2, no. 1, 2007, p. 90.

9   For more on this, see Joys Hoi Yan Cheung, *Chinese Music and Translated Modernity in Shanghai, 1918–1937*, dissertation, University of Michigan, 2008, p. 292.

10 Yik-man Edmond Tsang, *Beethoven in China: The Reception of Beethoven's Music and its Political Implications, 1949–1959*, thesis, University of Hong Kong, 2003, p. 53.

11 Ching-chih Liu, *A Critical History of New Music in China*, The Chinese University Press, Hong Kong, 2010, p. 66.

12 For more on this, see Mark O'Neill, *The Chinese Labour Corps*,

Penguin, Melbourne, 2014.

13 Mao Zedong, 'The May Fourth Movement', *Selected Works of Mao Zedong*, May 1939.

14 Lu Xun, 'Essay Number 46' (1919), as quoted in Shih Shumei, *The Lure of the Modern: Writing Modernism in Semi-Colonial China, 1917–1937*, University of California Press, Berkeley & Los Angeles, 2001, p. 73.

15 Shih Shumei, *The Lure of the Modern: Writing Modernism in Semi-Colonial China, 1917–1937*, University of California Press, Berkeley & Los Angeles, 2001, p. 75.

16 Paul B. Foster, *Ah Q Archaeology: Lu Xun, Ah Q, Ah Q Progeny, and the National Character Discourse in Twentieth Century China*, Lexington Books, Lanham, 2008, p. 77.

17 Leo Ou-fan Lee, *The Romantic Generation of Modern Chinese Writers*, Harvard University Press, Cambridge, 1973, pp. 156–7.

18 Liu, *A Critical History of New Music in China*, p. 183.

19 Tsang, *Beethoven in China*, p. 56.

20 George Alexander Fischer, *Beethoven: A Character Study*, 1905, republished by Desmondous Publications, 2015, p. 145.

21 Hong-yu Gong, 'Music, Nationalism, and the Search for Modernity in China, 1911–1949', *New Zealand Journal of Asian Studies*, vol. 10, no. 2, December 2008, p. 60.

22 Liu, *A Critical History of New Music in China*, p. 174.

23 Col. Sir Henry Rule (trans. and ed.), *Cathay and the Way Thither. Being a Collection of Medieval Notices of China*, revised ed. by Henri Cordier, 4 vol., London 1913–1916, republished by Ch'eng-wen Publishing Co., Taipei, vol. 3, 1966, pp. 46–47.

24 Sheila Melvin and Jindong Cai, *Rhapsody in Red*, Algora Publishing, 2004, p. 65.

25 W.S. Pakenham-Walsh, 'Foochow Easter Monday Choral Festival', *The Chinese Recorder and Missionary Journal*, vol. 39, American Presbyterian Press, 1908, p. 346.

26 Allen Artz Wiant, *A New Song for China*, Trafford Publishing, 1 January 2003, pp. 10–11.

27 Annual Report of the Shanghai Municipal Council, 1906, Band Report, p. 204.

28 Annual Report of the Shanghai Municipal Council, 1906, Band Report, p. 199.

29 Annual Report of the Shanghai Municipal Council, 1906, Band Report, p. 201.

30 Mengyu Luo, Shanghai Symphony Orchestra in 'C' Major (1879–2010), doctoral thesis, Loughboro University, 2013, pp. 93–94.

31 Melvin & Cai, *Rhapsody in Red*, p. 43.

32 Mario Paci, *Maestro Mario Paci*, souvenir program of farewell concert, Shanghai Municipal Orchestra, 31 May, pp. 13–15.

33 'Calls Beethoven a True Democrat, Governor Smith Praises Composers Universality in Message Sent to Celebration Here, Foreign Consuls Attend', *New York Times*, 26 March 1927.

34 Melvin & Cai, *Rhapsody in Red*, 2004, pp. 90–91.

35 Liu, *A Critical History of New Music in China*, p. 100.

36 Cheung, *Chinese Music and Translated Modernity in Shanghai, 1918–1937*, pp. 293–295.

37 Cheung, *Chinese Music and Translated Modernity in Shanghai, 1918–1937*, pp. 293–295.

38 Chen Pingyuan, *Touches of History: An Entry into 'May Fourth' China*, Brill, 2011, p. 161.

39 Chen Pingyuan, *Touches of History*, p. 181.

40 Gong, 'Music, Nationalism, and the Search for Modernity in China, 1911–1949', pp. 43–50.

41 Tsang, *Beethoven in China*, p. 71.

42 Chen Pingyuan, *Touches of History*, p. 184.

43 Chen Pingyuan, *Touches of History*, p. 184.

44 Chen Pingyuan, *Touches of History*, p. 194.

45 Gong, 'Music, Nationalism, and the Search for Modernity in China, 1911–1949', p. 31.

46 Gong, 'Music, Nationalism, and the Search for Modernity in China, 1911–1949', p. 47.

47 Gong, 'Music, Nationalism, and the Search for Modernity in China, 1911–1949', p. 47.

48 Gong, 'Music, Nationalism, and the Search for Modernity in China, 1911–1949', p. 48.

49 Gong, 'Music, Nationalism, and the Search for Modernity in China, 1911–1949', p. 48.

50 Zhang Lexin, *Beethoven in China* (贝多芬在中国), Central Conservatory Publishing House (中央音乐学院出版社), Beijing, 2013, p. 75.

51 Melvin & Cai, *Rhapsody in Red*, p. 215.

52 Liu, *A Critical History of New Music in China*, p. 90.

53 R.B. Hurry, 'A Far Eastern Gateway', *Music and Letters*, vol. 3, no. 4, 1922, p. 372.

54 Luo, *Shanghai Symphony Orchestra in 'C' Major (1879–2010)*, p. 76.

55 Tsang, *Beethoven in China*, p. 57.

56 Jin Mei, *Biography of Fu Lei* (傅雷传), Hunan Wenyi Publishing House (湖南文艺出版社), 1993, p. 6.

57 Cheung, *Chinese Music and Translated Modernity in Shanghai, 1918–1937*, p. 209.

58 Stefan Zweig (translated by Eden Paul & Cedar Paul), *Romain Rolland: The Man and His Work*, Thomas Seltzer, New York, 1921, p. 140.

59 Cited in Alexander Wheelock Thayer & Elliot Forbes (eds), *Thayer's Life of Beethoven*, Princeton University Press, 1991, p. 305.

60 Romain Rolland (translated by Constance Hull), *Beethoven*, Library of Music and Musicians, London, 1930, p. 80.

61 Tian Chuanmao, 'Fu Lei's Translation Activity and Legacy', *Journal of Language and Culture*, vol. 2, no. 10, 2011, pp. 174–183.

62 Fu Lei, preface to *Life of Beethoven* (贝多芬传), Shanghai Camel Bookstore (上海骆驼书店), 1946.

63 Huang Yuanfan, 'Tragedy and Triumph of a Chinese Intellectual', *Global Times*, 31 October 2013.

64 Miao Jun & Andre Salem, *The Specificity of Translator's Notes, Textometrical Analysis of Footnotes in Fu Lei's Translation of Jean-Christophe by Romain Rolland*, Using Corpora in Contrastive and Translation Studies, Zhejiang University, September 2008, p. 26.

65 *The Nation*, vol. 93, 14 December 1911, p. 575.

66 Romain Rolland, *Jean-Christophe*, Volume 1.

67 Miao Jun & Andre Salem, *The Specificity of Translator's Notes, Textometrical Analysis of Footnotes in Fu Lei's Translation of Jean-Christophe by Romain Rolland*, p. 26.

68 Theo Hermans, *Crosscultural Transgressions: Research Models in Translation: V. 2: Historical and Ideological Issues*, Routledge, 10 July 2014, p. 159.

69 Allen Artz Wiant, *A New Song for China*, Trafford Publishing, 2003.

70 Andrew Jones, *Yellow Music: Media Culture and Colonial Modernity in the Chinese Jazz Age*, Duke University Press, 2001, p. 106.

71 Mao Zedong, 'Talks at the Yan'an Forum on Literature and Art', in *Mao Tse-Tung on Literature and Art*, Peking, Foreign Languages Press, 1977, p. 25.

72 Leo Ou-fan Lee, *Shanghai Modern: The Flowering of a New Urban Culture in China, 1930–1945*, Harvard University Press, 1999, p. 230.

73 Translated by Jong Lester & A. C. Barnes, quoted in Shannon Elizabeth Reed, *The New Romantics: Romantic Themes in the Poetry of Guo Moruo and Xu Zhimo*, thesis, William and Mary, 2009.

74 Mao Zedong, 'On the People's Democratic Dictatorship (1949)', *Selected Works of Mao Zedong*, vol. 4.

75   Mao Zedong, 'On the People's Democratic Dictatorship (1949)', *Selected Works of Mao Zedong*, vol. 4.

76   Maynard Solomon (ed.), *Marxism and Art: Essays Classic and Contemporary*, Wayne State University Press, 1974, p. 163.

77   Solomon (ed.), *Marxism and Art: Essays Classic and Contemporary*, p. 164.

78   V. I. Lenin, 'Krupskaya and Lenin to Lenin's Mother (December 26, 1913)', *Collected Works*, vol. 37, Progress Publishers, Moscow, 1977, pp. 507–508.

79   In Arnold Perris, 'Music as Propaganda: Art at the Command of Doctrine in the People's Republic of China', *Ethnomusicology*, vol. 27, no. 1, 1983, pp. 1–28.

80   Maxim Gorky, 'V. I. Lenin', Lenin Museum and Maxim Gorky Internet Archive (www.marxists.org/archive/gorky-maxim/1924/01/x01.htm).

81   Leon Botstein, 'Art and the State: The Case of Music', *Musical Quarterly*, vol. 88, no. 4, 2005, p. 489. This was even though, Botstein notes, Beethoven's 'major source of economic support throughout his life was direct subvention by a small group of connoisseurs who were members of the landed aristocracy'.

82   Yelena Muratova, 'Beethoven the Soviet Revolutionary', *UCLA Journal of Slavic and East European/Central Studies*, vol. 7, 2014–15, p. 1.

83   Muratova, 'Beethoven the Soviet Revolutionary', p. 5.

84   Amy Nelson, *Music for the Revolution: Musicians and Power in Early Soviet Russia*, Penn State Press, 2010, p. 186.

85   Nelson, *Music for the Revolution*, p. 189.

86   Tsang, *Beethoven in China*, p. 84.

87   Tsang, *Beethoven in China*, pp. 92–93.

88   David B. Dennis, *Beethoven in German Politics, 1870–1989*, Yale University Press, 1996, p. 41.

89   Tsang, *Beethoven in China*, p. 92.

90   Zhou Guangzhen, *A History of the Central Philharmonic* (中央乐团史), Joint Publishing (三联), Hong Kong, 2009, p. 676. For description of the 'Pastoral', see Rolland, *Vie de Beethoven*, p. 120.

91   Tsang, *Beethoven in China*, p. 101.

92   Richard Curt Kraus, *Pianos and Politics in China*, Oxford University Press, 1989, p. 75.

93   Mao Yurun, 'Music under Mao, Its Background and Aftermath', *Asian Music*, vol. 22, no. 2, 1991, p. 106.

94   Liu Wenzhong, 'Austria – Remembering Lu Hongen, my friend in shared suffering', *Xinhai Guotuzhi* (新海国图志), July 2009 (*http://blog.sina.com.cn/s/blog_4c288f1b0100e4vx.html*).

95   Melvin & Cai, *Rhapsody in Red*, p. 218.

96   Mao Yurun, 'Music under Mao', p. 113.

97   Oliver Chou, 'Band of Hope and Glory: Dresden Philharmonic's Ties with Mao', *South China Morning Post Magazine*, 20 October 2013.

98   Zhou Guangzhen, *A History of the Central Philharmonic*, pp. 129–130.

99   Zhou Guangzhen, *A History of the Central Philharmonic*, p. 130.

100 'National Day Echoes', *Peking Review*, 13 October 1959, p. 4.

101 Chou, 'Band of Hope and Glory'.

102 'German Art and Artists in Peking', *Peking Review*, 20 October 1959, p. 18.

103 'German Art and Artists in Peking,' p. 18.

104 Chou, 'Band of Hope and Glory'.

105 Chou, 'Band of Hope and Glory'.

106 Tsang, *Beethoven in China*, p. 113.

107 Frederick Page, 'Music in China', *The Musical Times*, vol. 104, no. 1443, 1963, pp. 331–332.

108 Robert Guillian, 'China Revisited', *The World Today*, vol. 21, no. 3, 1965, pp. 101–111.

109 Luo, *Shanghai Symphony Orchestra in 'C' Major (1879–2010)*, p. 188.

110 Melvin & Cai, *Rhapsody in Red*, p. 233.

111 Gail Jennes, 'Pianist Liu Shih-Kun Wins Bravos in Boston After Years of Forced Silence in a Peking Prison', *People Magazine*, 16 April 1979.

112 Jun Liu, 'Beacon of Light for Many', *China Daily*, 15 April 2008, and Jiaqi Yan & Gao Gao, *Turbulent Decade: A History of the Cultural Revolution*, University of Hawaii Press, 1996, p. 80.

113 Fu Lei's letter is reproduced in *Centennial Commemoration of Fu Lei*, Beijing Library Publishing House, 2008, p. 234.

114 Liu Wenzhong, 'Austria – Remembering Lu Hongen, my friend in shared suffering'.

115 'Missa Solemnis in D Major, Op. 123', The Kennedy Center (http://m.kennedy-center.org/home/program/5037).

116 Zweig, *Romain Rolland*, pp. 141–142.

117 Barbara Mittler, '"Enjoying the Four Olds!" Oral Histories from a "Cultural Desert"', *Transcultural Studies*, No. 1, University of Heidelberg, 2013.

118 Melvin & Cai, *Rhapsody in Red*, p. 266.

119 Henry Kissinger, *Years of Upheaval: The Second Volume of His Classic Memoirs*, Simon & Schuster, 2011.

120 Melvin & Cai, *Rhapsody in Red*, p. 274.

121 Luo, *Shanghai Symphony Orchestra in 'C' Major (1879–2010)*, p. 408.

122 'Notebook, London Philharmonic', *Peking Review*, 30 March 1973, p. 19.

123 Francis B. Tenny, 'The Philadelphia Orchestra's 1973 China Tour', *American Diplomacy*, September 2012.

124 Nicholas Platt, *China Boys: How U. S. Relations with the PRC Began and Grew, A Personal Memoir*, ADST-DACOR Diplomats and Diplomacy Series, Washington DC, 2009, Chapter 17.

125 'Philadelphia Orchestra in Peking', p. 11.

126 H. Schonberg, 'Ormandy, Unexpectedly, Leads Peking Orchestra', *New York Times*, 16 September 1973.

127 Hua Chao, 'Has Absolute Music No Class Character?', *Peking Review*, No. 9, 1 March 1974, pp. 15–17.

128 'China Assails Beethoven and Schubert', *New York Times*, 15 January 1974.

129 See Kraus, *Pianos and Politics in China*, p. 237. (Original source is Verbatim Record of Chairman Mao's Talks with Comrade Deng Xiaoping in early July 1975. Document of Central Committee 15: 101 February 1979).

130 See Zhou Guangzhen, *A History of the Central Philharmonic*, pp. 362–363.

131 Lebrecht, Norman, 'A New Cultural Revolution', *Standpoint*, October 2013.

132 See Josiah Fisk and Jeff William Nichols, *Composers on Music, Eight Centuries of Writings*, UPNE, 1997, p. 55.

133 Tim Brook, 'The Revival of China's Musical Culture', *The China Quarterly*, No. 77, 1979, p. 116.

134 Page, 'A Musician in China', pp. 31–32.

135 Jane Glover, 'Across the Cultural Divide: Mozart in China', *RSA Journal*, vol. 137, no. 5394, 1989, p. 356.

136 Deborah Caulfield, *Los Angeles Times*, 20 April 1988.

137 Paul Theroux, *Riding the Iron Rooster*, New York, G.P. Putnam & Sons, 1988, pp. 422.

138 Heinrich Fruehauf, 'Urban Exoticism', in Ellen Widmer & Wang Te-wei, *From May Fourth to June Fourth: Fiction and Film in Twentieth-Century China*, Harvard University Press, 2009, p. 154.

139 Fu Guangming, 'Beethoven's Music and the Spirit of Modern Chinese Writers', 23 March 2012 (http://blog.sina.com.cn/s/blog_4adc338c01011x7v.html).

140 Ting Wai, 'Human Rights and EU-China Relations', in Roland Vogt (ed.), *Europe and China: Strategic Partners or Rivals*, Hong Kong University Press, 2012.

141 Zhou Guangzhen, *A History of the Central Philharmonic*, p. 512.

142 See Greg Mitchell, 'Tiananmen Square Massacre: How Beethoven Rallied the Students', 14 November 2013 (http://billmoyers.com/content/tiananmen-square-massacre-how-beethoven-rallied-the-students/).

143 See Edward Wong, 'Repackaging the Revolutionary Classics of China', *New York Times*, 29 June 2011.

144 Xu Jingxi, 'On Beethoven's Back', *China Daily*, 29 May 2014.

145 See Beethoven-Haus, Bonn, Digital Archives (http://www.beethoven-haus-bonn.de/sixcms/detail.php?id=&template=dokseite_digitales_archiv_en&_dokid=bi:i2987&_seite=1).

146 Rolland, *Vie de Beethoven*, p. 51–52.

PHOTOGRAPHS

All photographs provided by Jindong Cai and Sheila
Melvin except where indicated below:

P33, 74 Shanghai Symphony Orchestra
P76, 103 China National Symphony Orchestra
P104 Philadelphia Orchestra
P87 China Friendship Publishing Company
（中国友谊出版公司）

The Penguin China Specials:
First World War Series

The First World War may well have been the twentieth century's most significant event, its myriad ripple effects and consequences are still being felt today. However, to date, it has mostly been seen from a European perspective, images of brave, young soldiers in the trenches have, quite rightly, been seared deep on the collective consciousness of the West and their sacrifice should never be forgotten. That said, as with most things in life, the war was far more complex than that and it led – both directly and indirectly – to the Bolshevik Revolution in Russia, the May Fourth Movement in China and Japanese imperialism in the Far East, as well as, of course, the Second World War and its resulting Cold War. To mark its centenary Penguin is publishing a series of Specials which will look at the conflict from a different perspective.

If you enjoyed this Penguin China Special why not try another in the First World War series:

The Siege of Tsingtao: The only battle of the First World War to be fought in Asia by Jonathan Fenby

The Chinese Labour Corps: The Forgotten Chinese Labourers of the First World War by Mark O'Neill

Betrayal in Paris: How the Treaty of Versailles Led to China's Long Revolution by Paul French

Getting Stuck in for Shanghai by Robert Bickers

From the Tsar's Railway to the Red Army: The Experience of Chinese Labourers in Russia During the First World War and Bolshevik Revolution by Mark O'Neill

Picnics Prohibited: China in the First World War by Frances Wood

England's Yellow Peril: Sinophobia and the Great War by Anne Witchard

PENGUIN
SPECIALS

What's Wrong with Diplomacy?

KERRY BROWN

The Future of Diplomacy and the Case of China and the UK

As Xi Jinping assumes the presidency during China's biggest leadership transition in decades, the Communist top brass are finding it increasingly difficult to keep their poisonous internal divisions behind closed doors. The breathtaking — and politically convenient — fall from grace of Xi's long-time rival Bo Xilai is an extraordinary tale of excess, defection, political purges and ideological clashes going back to Mao himself. But it was the conviction of Bo's wife for murder of an Englishman that enabled the destruction of his reputation. Our leading China correspondent, John Garnaut, reveals a particularly Chinese spin on the old adage that the personal is political.

Kerry Brown is Professor of Chinese Politics and Director of the China Studies Centre at the University of Sydney, and Associate Fellow on the Asia Programme at Chatham House, London. He served in the British Foreign and Commonwealth Office from 1998 to 2005, and is the author of over ten books, the most recent being *The New Emperors: Power* and the *Princelings in Modern China*.